Ron,

You have become one of the most influencial people in life through the story you live out day to day. Thank you for speaking truth & grace into my story which has helped me in more deeper ways than I ever could express.

This book is the poetic story of God's Eternal Love - read it and be filled with His Wonder.

In

SPIRITUAL LIFE

THE DIVINE DRAMA

THE DIVINE DRAMA

⊕ ⊕ ⊕

KURT BRUNER

TYNDALE HOUSE PUBLISHERS, INC.
WHEATON, IL

Library of Congress Cataloging-in-Publication Data

Bruner, Kurt D.
   The divine drama / Kurt Bruner.
      p. cm.
Includes bibliographical references.
ISBN 0-8423-3839-X (hardcover)
I. Christian life.   2. Economy of God.   3. Narrative theology.   I. Title.
BV4509.5 .B74 2001
230—dc2I   2001004106

Printed in the United States of America

06   05   04   03   02   0I
7   6   5   4   3   2   I

CONTENTS

PROLOGUE

LIFE is best understood through a story—God's story. It is a story that transcends and explains our experiences, our questions, our deepest yearnings, our greatest hurts.

It is about God the person. His passions. His hopes. His heart.

It is a story that includes a cherished beloved, a seductive villain, a hero's journey, and a broken heart.

It begins with "Once upon a time" and ends with "happily ever after."

It is a story within which our own can be told.

INTRODUCTION

⊕ ⊕ ⊕

WE LOVE *Romeo and Juliet* because it's a passionate love story. We love *The Lord of the Rings* because it's a fantastic adventure. We love *Sherlock Holmes* because it's suspenseful mystery. We love *The Hunchback of Notre Dame* because it's touching tragedy. We love *Rocky* because a nice underdog wins, and we love *Star Wars* because an evil villain loses. We love the gospel because it is all of the above.

There is an epic drama unfolding on the stage of time. You and I are part of the cast. The play is written and directed by the Almighty himself. Every line, every scene, every twist, and every turn will culminate in the most amazing and satisfying conclusion ever performed. It is the tale all others seek to tell. Every love story was inspired by its romance; every adventure, its quest; every tragedy, its sorrow; and every comedy, its joy.

Shakespeare was right; our world *is* a stage—and each of us, a player. But in the drama of life, we make real choices with real consequences. The stakes are very high because, unlike any other play, this drama does more than merely portray life and death. It *is* life and death.

⊕ ⊕ ⊕

I've come to believe that the meaning of life can be found in story, and the meaning of story can be found in life. This book is about where life and story meet. And once that place is found, the story of your life may never be the same.

Think about the power of stories. They entertain us. They challenge us. They encourage us. They transform us. They can bring a smile, draw a tear, inspire hope, or arouse despair. A good story can ignite the flame of passion, mend the pain of a broken heart, calm an anxious spirit, or stir a passive soul. Who can resist curling up in that favorite chair with a good book, enjoying a large bucket of buttered popcorn while watching the latest big-screen movie hit, or sitting around the table with friends and loved ones as they tell tales of the past? Whatever form they may take, stories draw us like nothing else in life.

Good stories contain and explain the essence of human experience. And when written or performed well, a good story causes our emotions to quicken as we resonate with its telling. We cheer when the hero overtakes the villain. Our hearts rejoice when the guy finally gets the girl and they begin their "happily ever after." Despair turns to jubilation as the cavalry rides in at the darkest possible moment to save the day.

Have you ever wondered why, when so much of real life seems unhappy, we are so drawn to happy endings? We carry with us into every story a certain expectancy that, if not satisfied, makes us feel cheated. Every "Once upon a time" builds anticipation for the eventual "happily ever after." Each villain set upon destruction requires a virtuous hero committed to justice. A story that fails to fulfill these expectations is like an unresolved musical chord, leaving us tense, distressed, yearning for resolution.

Some would say this is because we're hopeless romantics—desiring what can't be possessed, seeking momentary escape from the harsh realities of life. But maybe, just maybe, there's a more compelling explanation—one that captures the imagination instead of insulting it. As fantasy fiction novelist J. R. R. Tolkien wrote, "Why should a man be scorned, if, finding himself in prison, he tries to get out and go home?" What if, rather than trying to escape reality, our spirits are trying to connect with it? What if good stories are good not because they distract our troubled hearts but because they affirm our deepest aspirations? What if the dramatic themes we love are actually reflections of a true, yet transcendent, story being told on the stage of life? What if there really is a brave hero fighting the forces of evil in order to save the world from destruction? What if there really is a handsome prince in pursuit of his princess, trying to free her from the evil clutches of a seductive villain? What if, just when all seems lost, the hero actually will break free and save the day? What if "Once upon a time" is truly progressing toward an eventual "happily ever after"? How would your own story change if you knew the plot of the larger story within which it is being told?

This book is about that story—the epic tale being written and produced by the omniscient Author of life. It's a story that provides a framework for the story of our own lives. It gives a window into the grand adventure unfolding throughout time and eternity, and it opens our eyes to the mystery and majesty of the transcendent drama in which we play a critical role.

I invite you to join me in discovering our part in God's story. First, we will examine the reality and importance of a drama that both transcends and explains the world we inhabit. Second, the Christian narrative will unfold scene by scene—from "Once upon a time" to "happily ever after"—in an effort to understand the main plot of the story of God.

Finally, in part three, we will explore how you and I fit into this epic tale.

My prayer is that the following pages will inspire your spirit and open your eyes. May they help you, like me, discover the place where life and story meet.

PART ONE

THE DIVINE DRAMA

A TRUE MYTH

I SUSPECT THAT MEN HAVE SOMETIMES
DERIVED MORE SPIRITUAL SUSTENANCE
FROM MYTHS THEY DID NOT BELIEVE
THAN FROM THE RELIGION THEY PROFESSED.
C. S. LEWIS

⊕ ⊕ ⊕

AFTER nearly thirty years of Christian faith, I found myself in a crisis of awareness and understanding that led to profound changes in how I view and experience the wonderful gift of life. I was raised in a strong Christian family. Attending Sunday school every week taught me all of the familiar Bible stories and memory verses. Three years in seminary added hermeneutics, apologetics, and systematics to my theological tool kit. Fifteen years working in Christian ministry gave me confidence in the art of applying biblical principles to the realities of everyday living. The end result? My Christianity was safe, certain, categorized, defensible, practical, predictable—and dry as dust.

None of the things I had learned or achieved filled that quiet but persistent yearning within. I expected my faith to do more than answer questions few seemed to ask. I wanted it to fill me with passion, adventure, risk, mystery, and wonder—none of which were in my life. It didn't make sense. I had in my possession the most meaningful and profound message in life but found it to be rather dull, uninteresting, ho-hum. I never doubted the truth of what I believed. It just seemed too small, like I had merely touched around the edges

3

of what is at the core of Christianity, never quite connecting with the deeper reality.

I knew there had to be more—just below the surface, slightly out of reach, or around the next corner, but definitely there. I felt like a blind man standing in a picture gallery, in the midst of something incredible and yet unable to partake of the rich beauty all around me.

Then came the crisis. It wasn't triggered by any kind of tragedy. In fact, my life had never been better—I had a wonderful wife, healthy and happy kids, a terrific job, a great church, and a better salary than I deserved. Nor was it caused by any kind of mysterious spiritual experience. I've never had one of those. There was no sudden bright light or voice in the middle of the night.

It didn't happen all at once but over time. This crisis was more of a process than a single event. Brief encounters here and there. None of them very dramatic but all of them reshaping the lenses through which I saw my life, my world, and my faith.

Like many who profess Christianity, I had done so without understanding exactly how my own life fit within the glorious story of God. I had learned to read the Bible as a collection of lessons and truths rather than the script of an epic drama that has been unfolding since before the dawn of time. I had failed to see history as more than a series of disconnected, random events or my life as part of anything bigger than my own routine.

THE CURTAIN RAISED

It was on a flight home from a business trip that my eyes began to open to the reality of the divine drama. After sorting through my usual stack of miscellaneous memos, reports, and articles, I picked up *The Writer's Journey: Mythic*

Structure for Storytellers and Screenwriters, a book by screenplay-writing instructor Christopher Vogler that had been recommended by a colleague. It was one of those titles on my "ought to" reading list. I would have preferred relaxing with the latest Grisham novel. But having recently accepted the responsibility of overseeing both film and radio drama projects for Focus on the Family, I now had the responsibility of approving or rejecting story concepts and scripts. Having little experience beyond an occasional Blockbuster rental or dollar-cinema selection, I decided to learn all I could about what makes a good story.

Using illustrations from dozens of films, Vogler revealed the common pattern found in some of the most popular movies ever produced—many of which I had enjoyed without really understanding why. If I was going to evaluate story ideas effectively, I needed to understand that pattern. So I continued reading in order to enhance my professional skills. What I discovered began a journey that changed my life.

The idea is simple and, at the same time, profound. All great stories adhere to the same basic structure. When that structure is followed, a story will inspire its readers. When it is ignored, the story will bore them. These common structural elements found universally in myths, fairy tales, fables, novels, and movies are known collectively as "the hero's journey."

What is the hero's journey? Put simply, it is the quest pursued by the central character of every story—be it Dorothy in *The Wizard of Oz,* Christian in *Pilgrim's Progress,* or Luke Skywalker in *Star Wars.* The same pattern of overcoming obstacles in pursuit of a desired object found in Tolkien's *The Lord of the Rings* can also be found in Disney's *Toy Story.* The heroic drives that motivate young Peter in Narnia also stir

King Arthur in Camelot. The settings, challenges, characters, and details are different as can be. But the journey is the same.

⊕ ⊕ ⊕

Despite the infinite varieties, every story starts with a hero— a central character living the familiar circumstances of whatever "ordinary life" he may know. But then something happens to throw life out of balance, calling the hero on a quest for some "object of desire." Overcoming many obstacles and challenges in pursuit of that object, the hero eventually faces an "ultimate confrontation" necessary to regain equilibrium in his life or world. In most cases the stakes continue to rise until the hero faces off with a supreme antagonist—up to and often including death itself. If the hero is willing to sacrifice something precious, perhaps his life, he can obtain the remedy needed to return his world to a state of harmony.

One example of this is the classic "guy meets girl" story. The hero (the guy) is perfectly content with his life until he encounters an object of desire (the girl). Suddenly "ordinary life" is no longer good enough. He's propelled into a quest, driven to face and overcome whatever obstacles are necessary to have the girl. Ultimately, he must "die" to the self-centered bachelor life if he hopes to win her heart and resurrect harmony in his life.

Another example of the hero's journey is the action-adventure story. The hero is living the "ordinary life" of crime fighter, soldier, or secret agent when an ominous villain enters the picture—perhaps his old nemesis. Before you know it, the hero is risking his life in order to save the world from some great danger. He "dies" to self-preservation in order to defeat the villain's threat. Sometimes he is literally killed, other times he is merely injured. But he always gives up something in order to win the day.

If a story does not follow the pattern of the hero's journey, it fails to connect with our spirits. Imagine how popular the *Rocky* series would have been had Rocky Balboa remained home instead of fighting Apollo Creed. If he hadn't taken the hero's journey, there would have been no conflict, no victory, and no audience. What if Peter, Edmund, Lucy, and Susan played their game of hide-and-seek without entering the world of Narnia? They would never have encountered the dangers of the White Witch, the wonder of King Aslan, or any of the adventures millions have enjoyed in *The Chronicles of Narnia*, by C. S. Lewis. The importance of this pattern is clear to Hollywood. Embracing the mythic power of the hero's journey enabled Walt Disney to capture the hearts (and wallets) of an entire generation. Screenplay writers and producers create box-office hits each year through this classic story structure. They know that films using it will find an audience. Those that don't, won't.

⊕ ⊕ ⊕

As we will discover in part two, the parallels between the hero's journey and the gospel narrative are striking. A hero leaves his ordinary world on a quest to face his old nemesis in order to obtain an object of desire. Overcoming great obstacles, he eventually faces death to remedy the problems of the world.

So if stories that reflect the mythic structure of the hero's journey resonate with people and our hearts yearn for the themes they portray, could it be that these yearnings are God given? Might they be pointing us to a story he wants us to encounter? Perhaps the stories we wish were true are those that reflect the story that *is* true.

While asking these questions, I came across an interview between journalist Bill Moyers and the late Joseph Campbell, author of *Hero with a Thousand Faces,* that brought the concept of the hero's journey to my attention. Campbell believed that the answer to man's search for meaning in life resides in every story, myth, legend, and fairy tale.

Raised in the Roman Catholic tradition and familiar with the gospel, Campbell discovered the themes and patterns residing within the Christian narrative pushing their way through the myths and stories of other cultures and religions. As he discovered the similarities, he began to connect the dots. His conclusion? That all of these stories, the Christian gospel included, reflect a deeper reality of what it means to be human. Campbell considered none of them, the Christian gospel included, necessarily true in an ultimate sense. He felt that it's what they reflect, not what they claim, that's important. Campbell placed Christ in the same category as Moses, Buddha, Mohammed, and every other religious "hero" on a journey. Since the "legend" of Jesus follows the same mythic structure as other great cultural or religious stories, he felt there must be a universal truth that all of them are trying to proclaim—but that none of them completely contain. From Campbell's perspective, they don't reflect that which is beyond us but that which is within us.

Obviously, I couldn't agree. Christ is unique, and the gospel is in a different category than any other story. I could not accept the notion that Jesus was just another mythic figure, or that his life, death, and resurrection were merely symbolic of every man's quest. But neither could I ignore the fact that other cultural stories, religious leaders, and heroes looked very similar to those described in the Christian worldview. I concluded that despite his flawed conclusion, Campbell must have encountered a piece of the truth. A truth that reinforced the existence of a universal, overarching story all others seek to tell. But as I later discovered, a truth missing the more important part.

⊕ ⊕ ⊕

As one who came into Christianity having already immersed himself in the rich world of classic literature, myths, legends, and fables, C. S. Lewis had unique insight into the obvious parallels existing among various religious and cultural traditions. Like Campbell, he recognized the similarities in their myths and stories. Unlike Campbell, he saw them as a reflection of the Christian gospel rather than an alternative to it. Responding to the suggestion that the images and story of Christ aren't as important as the lessons he taught, Lewis defended the gospel narrative as critical to true Christian faith—and to understanding ultimate reality.

> *The heart of Christianity is a myth which is also a fact. . . . It happens—at a particular date, in a particular place, followed by definable historical consequences. . . . By becoming fact it does not cease to be myth: that is the miracle.* (God in the Dock, 66-67)

Our generation typically uses the word *myth* to describe a story that's not true. Lewis used the word in the classic sense—to describe a story that reflects universal truth. In this context, Christianity is the supreme myth—the true, transcendent story that all others are modeled after. According to Lewis, we should not be surprised when other cultures, legends, and myths reflect our hero's journey. We should be surprised when they don't. If ours is the true myth, it seems likely that a yearning within all men would point them to a story that is also history. If the pattern of the gospel resides within the human heart, it should push its way out in the stories we tell.

Lewis wasn't alone in his view that the stories we love reflect the true story of the gospel. His colleague and close friend J. R. R. Tolkien created what became the most popular fantasy of the twentieth century, *The Lord of the Rings*. The world he created, Middle-earth, is one in which hobbits, elves, dwarfs, and men battle side by side to overcome an evil that threatens to destroy their way of life. It also reflects a greater reality, a true hero's journey revealed in Tolkien's Christian faith. In his essay entitled "On Fairy-Stories," Tolkien identified the gospel narrative of Christ's life, death, and resurrection as the ultimate fairy-story.

> *The Gospels contain a fairy-story, or a story of a larger kind which embraces all the essence of fairy-stories. They contain many marvels—particularly artistic, beautiful, and moving: "mythical" in their perfect, self-contained significance. . . . But this story has entered History and the primary world. . . . This story is supreme; and it is true. Art has been verified. God is the Lord, of angels, and of men—and of elves. ("On Fairy-Stories," 71–72)*

Another contemporary of Lewis, playwright Dorothy Sayers, wrote this:

> *For Jesus Christ is unique—unique among gods and men. There have been incarnate gods a-plenty, and slain-and-resurrected gods not a few; but He is the only God who has a date in history. (Sayers, 20)*

Lewis, Tolkien, Sayers, and others recognized, like Campbell, the pattern residing within the great myths and folklore of all cultures. Unlike Campbell, however, they did not see this pattern as undermining the Christian gospel. Rather, they felt that it affirms the truth of the Christian gospel—a truth based upon something much more profound than mere human experience. A truth based upon the greatest story ever told, written by God himself.

My journey led me into several life-changing discoveries: First, there is an overarching structure to every great story. Second, this structure satisfies yearnings residing deep within the human heart. Third, the stories we wish were true reveal a void that can be filled only by the one story that is true. Finally, the gospel is the drama of a hero's quest—a hero who entered history in the person of Jesus Christ.

Sadly, many who have embraced the reality of Christ have missed the story. I did. Having my theological ducks in a row may have informed my mind, but it did little to inspire my heart. Somehow I missed the drama of the gospel, experiencing more passion watching Luke Skywalker on a quest to defeat Darth Vader than I did watching Christ on his quest to defeat death.

Perhaps Hollywood is more in tune with the adventure and wonder of our story than we are. We know the fact but miss the myth. They know the myth but miss the fact. Is it any wonder one side is bored while the other is bewildered?

If the world is a stage and we are the actors, then life can only make sense when we understand the plot to the story being told. Toward that end, I began to wrestle with the questions we all ask in one form or another: Who is the author of this drama? What part does he want me to play? Am I the star of my own story or a supporting actor in someone else's? Who are the good guys and who are the bad guys? What kind of story is it? a romance? a comedy? a tragedy? a fairy tale? Will it have a happy or a sad ending?

The answers to these questions began to infuse my pale, black-and-white world with rich, full color. Life took on new meaning when I began to see it as part of something much bigger than the mundane details of daily living. The simple gospel I had embraced as a child invaded every other area of my life. I began to experience the wonderful adventure that had always been there, but that I had been unable or unwilling to see. The curtain had finally been raised, revealing that I was part of a divine drama.

The things I was missing—passion, adventure, mystery, and wonder—found their way into my life as I began to see every moment of every day in the context of an epic tale being told on the stage of time and eternity.

PLOT OVER PROPOSITION

I grew up attending churches that placed a high priority on expository teaching. Each Sunday the pastor would take his place behind the pulpit and invite the congregation to "Open your Bibles to" whatever passage was his main sermon text. That was our cue that we could expect the next thirty to forty minutes to include three points, a poem, two application lessons, four yawns, a few glances at the watch, and the unspoken but all-important question: "When will this end?"

If you've attended many church services in your day, you have probably had a similar experience. It isn't that we don't want to listen, learn, and grow in our spiritual walk. We just bore easily listening to principles and puns.

Contrast this reality with what happens when you hear the phrase "Once upon a time." Rather than three points, a poem, and "When will this end?" you expect adventure, conflict, good guys, bad guys, and romance. Some stories draw a smile, others a tear. But they always hold our attention with the unspoken but all-important question: *"How* will this end?"

Broadcasting legend Paul Harvey, reflecting upon the power of art over argument, penned these words:

Nobody could have persuaded a generation of Americans to produce a baby boom—yet Shirley Temple movies made every couple want to have one. Military enlistments were lagging for our Air Force until, almost overnight, a movie called Top Gun had recruits standing in line. The power of art over argument.

Harvey goes on to explain how several great books of the nineteenth century had a dramatic impact upon their time. For example, British sweatshops for children thrived until Charles Dickens wrote about them—turning public sentiment. American slavery ended only after Harriet Beecher Stowe's book *Uncle Tom's Cabin* sold hundreds of thousands of copies—giving the struggling abolitionist movement the attention and support it needed. Even Abraham Lincoln credited Stowe with starting the Civil War. The classic *Black Beauty* led to statutes requiring more humane treatment of draft horses. And in another instance,

Once upon a time, a cartoonist named Walt Disney created an animal character called Bambi and, in one year, deer hunting nose-dived from a $5.7 million business to $1 million. The power of art over argument.

Is it any wonder that Hollywood has such an enormous impact upon our generation? It's much easier to hold the attention of a culture with "Once upon a time" than it is with "Open your Bibles to." The irony is that the Bible is the ultimate "Once upon a time" story filled with plots, subplots, and dramatic themes only faintly captured on the stage or the silver screen. The twists and turns reflected in the gospel are far more compelling than any novel ever to appear on *The New York Times* bestseller list.

Somewhere along the way, we as Christians have become so focused on the lessons that we have lost the story—missing the forest for the trees. Our presentation of the gospel often lacks inspiration and passion because we limit our theology to proposition and proof while neglecting its plot. We put an artificial wall between the profound realities of God and the exciting adventures of drama. Take our institutions of theological training, for example. Seminaries are almost exclusively dedicated to the exploration of propositional statements of truth. It's a rare school of theology that integrates the performing arts into a divinity curriculum. The two are kept quite separate, and it shows.

As a seminary graduate, I still have dozens of systematic theology books on my shelf. Preparing for a lecture on the love and holiness of God, I began rereading my theology books, hoping to find something that would help me relay profound and inspiring realities. What I discovered may have been profound, but it was hardly inspiring. For example, here is how the love of God was defined:

The immanent love of God is a rational and voluntary affection grounded in perfect reason and deliberate choice. Since God's love is rational, it involves a subordination of the emotional element to higher law than itself, namely, that of truth and holiness. (Bancroft, 77)

And on the holiness of God:

Holiness is self-affirming purity. In virtue of this attribute of His nature, God eternally wills and maintains His own moral excellence. (Bancroft, 77)

Don't get me wrong. I have nothing against precise definitions or propositional statements. It just seems that there must be a better way to reflect realities so deep and personal as God's love and holiness—truths that should inspire tears and terror, not yawns and apathy.

In the introduction to *The Man Born to Be King*, a series of plays portraying the life of Christ, Dorothy Sayers observes that "there is no more searching test of a theology than to submit it to dramatic handling; nothing so glaringly exposes inconsistencies in a character, a story, or a philosophy as to put it upon the stage and allow it to speak for itself." Her famous plays on the life of Christ did that very thing, showing just how coherent our theology is. She taught that depiction can be much more meaningful than description as a means of experiencing and expressing our theology.

⊕ ⊕ ⊕

In 1998 I was invited to participate in a prerelease screening of the animated feature *Prince of Egypt*, the first to be produced by the relatively new DreamWorks studio. The project was under the creative oversight of executive producer Jeffrey Katzenberg, the man responsible for reviving the art of full-length animated features at Disney. His earlier hits, such as *The Little Mermaid* and *The Lion King*, placed him on top of the family entertainment world. Now part of a new studio, Katzenberg and his team of more than four hundred artists worked four years to produce a masterpiece of biblical proportions.

After touring the studio for a behind-the-scenes overview of the production process, I sat down in the DreamWorks screening room with about thirty others for the moment of truth—a viewing of the almost-finished project. For the next ninety minutes, I sat in a darkened room experiencing the collective creative effort of writers, musicians, actors, animators, and special-effect specialists. From the opening note of the musical score to the final credits, my heart was captured by the story portrayed.

During the scene in which Moses meets God at the burning bush, I found myself in awe. Moses, responding to God's command that he confront Pharaoh and lead God's people to freedom, objects on the grounds that he is incompetent. "You've chosen the wrong messenger. How can I even speak to these people?" Seconds later, Moses is cowering in the corner like a frightened child as the voice of God bellows forth, "Who made man's mouth? Who made the deaf, the mute, the seeing, or the blind? Did not I? Now go!" In that dramatic moment, I could feel the wrath of God as something real and personal, completely justified while utterly terrifying. The tension lingered for a moment until, in a much softened tone, the presence of God surrounds Moses to gently lift him up from the ground while whispering tenderly into his frightened ear, "Oh, Moses. I shall be with you when you go to the king of Egypt. But Pharaoh will not listen. So I will stretch out my hand and smite Egypt with all my wonders." Comforted by the compassion and affirmation of God's love, Moses' eyes are suddenly opened to a power and majesty he has never known, light and wind surrounding him to create a scene of unparalleled splendor.

Moses, and we in the audience, had encountered the God of holiness, wrath, comfort, and love. A lump in my throat, goose bumps on my skin, and tears in my eyes were a tangible connection to the emotions Moses must have felt. In less than five minutes the film producers had somehow managed to capture realities of God's character and majesty with a power that years of seminary training could not accomplish. How could that happen? The answer came a few minutes later as we participated in a postscreening question-and-answer session with the production team.

Convinced that producing this film must have grown out of an authentic spiritual journey, one member of the Christian press asked Katzenberg what this project meant to his own faith experience. A secular Jew who admits to being driven by money, Katzenberg was quick to debunk the notion that he had suddenly become religious. His simple comment was filled with meaning. "Look. We are storytellers. That's what we do."

In other words, it was not theological training or deep faith that enabled him to portray God as both holy and loving, angry and gentle. It was the art of storytelling that allowed him, a nonbeliever, to teach believers something about their own theology. In the movie God was portrayed as a person with the perfect balance between holiness and love. He had to be portrayed this way, or the story wouldn't work.

How could one who has no personal faith in God understand God's nature well enough to portray him better than those with decades of theological training? Simple. Stories are able to depict what words can merely describe. From Shakespeare to Spielberg, we most enjoy stories that capture the themes and characters found in the gospel—the ultimate drama, the myth that is also fact, the transcendent reality of life. Propositions are important because they stimulate the mind. But they often fail to touch the heart and soul. According to Jesus' greatest command, all three are vital: "Love the Lord your God with all your *heart* and with all your *soul* and with all your *mind*" (Matthew 22:37, emphasis added).

Great stories touch the heart, soul, and mind by reflecting the key themes of the gospel itself. *Romeo and Juliet,* for example, portrays the passion and problem of true love. Passion creates a yearning so deep that life for both Romeo and Juliet seems meaningless without the other. But there's a problem. Their families are enemies, keeping them apart. Eventually they invent a scheme in which both risk (and lose) their lives in hopes of being together. And while theirs was an immature passion, like Christ, this couple was so overcome with love that they were willing to face death itself in order to cross the chasm of separation. This plot of passionate love that must overcome obstacles of separation is the underlying theme of every great love story, from *Sleepless in Seattle* to *Titanic.*

Another key theme is the one that can be found in nearly every action-adventure film. In the *Star Wars* epic, we find an underdog fighting for good facing a powerful villain on the side of evil. Luke Skywalker and his rebel army seek to free the galaxy from the tyrannical oppression of Darth Vader and his Imperial forces. The conflict between a good underdog and a powerful villain reflects the reality of a universe in which a villain named Satan seeks to oppress God's good world with the tyranny of sin and death. This plot of good versus evil is the underlying theme of every great adventure story, from *Peter Pan* to *Harry Potter.*

Sacrifice is also a key element in good stories. Every good story has a hero who, on one level or another, must sacrifice himself on behalf of others. The movie *Braveheart* tells of one such hero. William Wallace was a simple man who led the people of Scotland in a battle against injustice and oppression. In the end, he was betrayed and handed over to torture and death. His courage in death, however, became the inspiration that led others to carry on the battle for eventual freedom. The essence of heroism is self-sacrifice.

The original and ultimate heroic plot is the story of Jesus Christ, who "humbled himself and became obedient to death—even death on a cross" (Philippians 2:8).

LIFE'S PLOT

If the gospel is better depicted than described, better understood through story than proposition, why didn't God reveal it to us that way? After all, if God is writing and directing an epic drama in which our lives play a part, shouldn't he let us in on it? In truth, that is precisely what he has done in the Scriptures. Though he didn't reveal every detail of the story, we do see some of the central concepts.

- We know that God is the author, director, and central character. We call that providence.

  Who has ever given to God, that God should repay him? For from him and through him and to him are all things. To him be the glory forever! Amen. (Romans 11:35-36)

- We know that we are free to choose whether and how we will play our part. We call that free will.

  This day I call heaven and earth as witnesses against you that I have set before you life and death, blessings and curses. Now choose life. (Deuteronomy 30:19)

- We know that the main plot to the story deals with love, peril, and rescue. We call that the gospel.

  For God so loved the world that he gave his one and only Son, that whoever believes in him shall not perish but have eternal life. (John 3:16)

What we don't know is how every scene of every subplot in this drama will unfold or how our parts impact the rest of the story. We call that mystery. It's this sense of mystery that turns our daily experiences and choices into a great adventure. The realization and awareness of this adventure infuses with meaning every circumstance we face, every encounter we have, and every decision we make. It places us smack in the middle of something bigger than ourselves.

Consider the images and themes God used to portray his

story in the Scriptures. None of these images entirely captures the profound depths of who he is and how we can relate to him, but they combine to tell a powerful tale. There is, for example, the image of God as sovereign King ruling over soldiers and subjects.

The Lord is enthroned as King forever. The Lord gives strength to his people; the Lord blesses his people with peace. (Psalm 29:10-11)

You are my King and my God, who decrees victories for Jacob. Through you we push back our enemies; through your name we trample our foes. (Psalm 44:4-5)

On his robe and on his thigh he has this name written: KING OF KINGS AND LORD OF LORDS. (Revelation 19:16)

The plot of this drama includes betrayal by a trusted confidant who incites rebellion against the King in hopes of claiming the throne for himself.

You said in your heart, "I will ascend to heaven; I will raise my throne above the stars of God. . . . I will make myself like the Most High." (Isaiah 14:13-14)

God is also described as the shepherd watching over his sheep. This touching account is filled with gentleness and compassion—the shepherd guiding his flock, caring for the needs of his sheep, and fending off predators as they graze.

The Lord is my shepherd, I shall not be in want. He makes me lie down in green pastures. (Psalm 23:1-2)

I am the good shepherd. The good shepherd lays down his life for the sheep. (John 10:11)

Eventually the shepherd must leave his whole flock in order to find a lost lamb that has wandered off into the wilderness.

If a man owns a hundred sheep, and one of them wanders away, will he not leave the ninety-nine on the hills and go to look for the one that wandered off? And if he finds it, I tell you the truth, he is happier about that one sheep than about the ninety-nine that did not wander off. In the same way your Father in heaven is not willing that any of these little ones should be lost. (Matthew 18:12-14)

One of the more prominent images of Scripture portrays God as a loving father and us as his children.

As a father has compassion on his children, so the Lord has compassion on those who fear him. (Psalm 103:13)

How great is the love the Father has lavished on us, that we should be called children of God! And that is what we are! (1 John 3:1)

He waits patiently for us to end our misguided folly, come to our senses, and return home.

Bring the best robe and put it on him. Put a ring on his finger and sandals on his feet. Bring the fattened calf and kill it. Let's have a feast and celebrate. For this son of mine was dead and is alive again; he was lost and is found. (Luke 15:22-24)

Perhaps the most compelling image used to reveal the relationship between God and humans is that of the relationship between husband and wife. In the Old Testament God is husband and Israel is his adulterous wife.

"I remember the devotion of your youth, how as a bride you loved me and followed me through the desert. . . . But you have lived as a prostitute with many lovers. . . . Return, faithless people," declares the Lord, "for I am your husband. I will choose you."
(Jeremiah 2:2; 3:1, 14)

In the New Testament, Christ is the bridegroom and the church is his bride.

"For this reason a man will leave his father and mother and be united to his wife, and the two will become one flesh." This is a profound mystery—but I am talking about Christ and the church. (Ephesians 5:31-32)

The divine Author wrote his masterwork using many images, themes, plots, and subplots. Again, no single one adequately reflects the epic saga of Christian theology. Each is needed to enrich the fabric of the whole.

Our privilege and responsibility is to experience this providential drama as both audience and cast. It is my hope that as you read this book you'll experience the story scene by scene, starting with "Once upon a time" and ending with "happily ever after," and through it, gain a better understanding of our theology as seen through the lens of plot. Admittedly inadequate, this book seeks to capture the main story line of eternity—giving the context in which our lives play a part. As cast, we will encounter the mystery of free will; each of us chooses the part we play in God's story. Once we've read the script, understanding the larger story, we're better able to grasp and reflect upon where and how our role fits. This infuses every moment of life with new meaning.

As we enter the theater of providence, we'll discover that the gospel is many things: It's a passionate love story, a fantastic adventure, and a suspenseful mystery. Author Frederick Buechner describes it as tragedy, comedy, and fairy tale. It is first a tragedy because in it we encounter heartbreak, pain, and sorrow. It is also a comedy because the ending is one of joy and redemption. And it is a fairy tale. In Buechner's words,

> *That is the Gospel, this meeting of darkness and light and the final victory of light. That is the fairy tale of the Gospel with, of course, the one crucial difference from all other fairy tales, which is that the claim made for it is that it is true, that it not only happened once upon a time but has kept happening ever since and is happening still. (Buechner, 90)*

As you encounter the story of God, my prayer is that your eyes may be opened to the wonderful place where life and story merge and that your life's "Once upon a time" will discover the "happily ever after" for which it was made.

PART TWO

THE STORY OF GOD

BEFORE a story can be explained, it must be told. Therefore, we'll begin by letting the Christian narrative speak for itself. Obviously, it would be impossible to capture every possible variation of its telling or every subplot it contains. The most we can hope to achieve in these few pages is to briefly reflect the main plot of its central characters. God is the hero; the drama begins and ends with him. Lucifer is the antagonist, personifying the story's conflict and giving voice to God's dilemma. Mankind is the third character, the central focus of the epic battle between a villain's conspiracy and a hero's quest.

In this section we will analyze the drama scene by scene, exploring the lush truths it contains. But first, we want to experience the story as if it were a children's fairy tale—reading it straight through from "Once upon a time" to "happily ever after," as with any other story. We'll resist the temptation to dissect its parts, allowing the plot of Christian belief to unfold.

And so, as the lights dim and the curtains are raised, I invite you to join me in the epic drama written and produced by the Author of life: the story of God.

ACT I
ONCE UPON A TIME

Scene One

Once upon a time God lived in perfect harmony,
   unity, and love.
Perfect harmony—for he ruled all that was.
Perfect unity—for he was the source of all truth
   and life.
Perfect love—for his very essence was so.
He was King of the universe. All was right.
   All was good.

Scene Two

God expressed himself through boundless creativity:
Painting beautiful scenes on the canvas of eternity.
Composing thrilling symphonies for the universe to
   perform.
Engineering a perfectly ordered cosmos.
Scripting epic dramas for the stage of life.
The divine artist at work in his gallery, every creation
   an expression of his passionate heart.

Scene Three

This good King built a spectacular city.
Its citizens were a host of servants—those to whom
   he had given the gift of life. He appointed leaders
   to direct his affairs and entrusted them with the
   capacity and authority necessary to rule throughout
   his domain.
Governed under the firm yet loving rule of the King,
   all citizens of this great city lived with an enduring
   sense of wonder, reverence, and peace.

Scene Four

There was a leader among the King's host who was exalted above all others, as the King had ordained him to be. Lucifer was a model of perfection, full of wisdom and beauty—for the King had made him so.

He was the King's most trusted servant, appointed guardian over the King's most cherished domain— that place reserved for his greatest work of love.

Scene Five

Filled with the insanity of pride, he who had been given most turned against the giver. No longer content to worship the King, Lucifer incited rebellion. "Why must there be only one God? Why must all bow to him alone? I will no longer serve, but rule. I will no longer submit my will. Yes, I will be like the Most High!"

Persuading many he governed to join him, he declared war.

It was a minor skirmish put down by the King's might, but it was a betrayal that pierced his heart. Demanding separation from the source of life, Lucifer gave birth to death.

Scene Six

Victim of his own folly, architect of his own fall, the traitor was banished from the King's court— moving from friend to foe, from love to hate, from servant to saboteur, from honor to shame.

Eager to strike back, he nurtured the bitter seed of vengeance within his darkened heart. "My day will come!"

Scene Seven

The bitter aftertaste of betrayal lingering still, the
King spoke.

"I desire one to love beyond all others, one to shower
with my favor, one with whom I can share my
heart."

Though surrounded by servants, the King yearned for
a bride.

One who would not be obliged to serve his position
but free to respond to his heart. Risking another
betrayal, the King sought a true love.

Scene Eight

Love breathed new life—life unlike all others.

He created a masterpiece after his own image, one
who was more than mere servant. She was made to
be the supreme object of the King's affection.

Made to be loved, free to love in return—or not to
love.

A living portrait of his own nature, God's cherished
beloved.

Scene Nine

Overflowing with excitement, the divine lover
proclaimed the passion of his heart.

"How I love her! She is priceless to me, precious
beyond words. My heart leaps as we walk in the
cool of the day. I ache for her to know my heart. I
made her to be loved and to love freely in return.
For with freedom comes pure devotion. She will
not be obliged but willingly drawn. Oh, how I love
those moments when hand in hand we share the
thrilling oneness of intimate hearts."

Scene Ten

The King gave his beloved a perfectly prepared home,
enfolding his cherished with spectacular beauty. He
showered her with gifts from his heart, placing her
in a garden filled with all that is good.

Every day was filled with the wonder of discovery
and the thrill of adventure, every moment warmed
by the haven of acceptance.

It was a place to walk and talk together, a place to
call home.

Paradise.

Scene Eleven

And so it was. Magnificent creativity achieved.
Royal domain established.
Rebellion thwarted. Rebel banished.
The King's beloved basking in his tender care.
All was made right. All was made good.

ACT II

VILLAIN'S PLOT

Scene One

In the depths of darkness, the rebel endured the
shame of bitter affliction. From the heart of
hatred he spoke to a legion of wavering loyalists,
seeking to inspire the hope of regaining what had
been lost.

"We are not defeated; the war has only just begun.
Better to reign in hell than serve in heaven! No
longer bound by the dictates of the Tyrant, we are
free to live in a world of our own making. We are
gods—rulers of our own destiny, liberators of all
who seek to be as they will rather than as he wills.
Doubt not, our day will come!"

The empty ravings of madness in desperate search for
an occasion to avenge his shame.

Scene Two

The King glanced at his beloved—more beautiful
than ever with the light of his gaze resting upon
her. Approaching softly with an unguarded heart,
he directed her attention to the magnificent works
around them—the regal strength of a mountain
range, the breathtaking luster of the setting sun,
and the gentle symphony of a breeze-blown forest.

"I made these for you. They are the expression of my
being. I crafted them before you were formed. I've
shared them with no other. Enjoy them. Each is a
symbol of my abiding affection. They are all
yours—save one." Receiving his gifts, she was
stirred by his majestic splendor and touched by his
tender heart.

Scene Three

From the throne of evil came a leap of devilish
    delight.
"What fortune! My opportunity for vengeance has
    arrived.
The Tyrant has foolishly given his heart to another.
Though I cannot defeat his might, perhaps I can
    subvert his love.
But by what means? By what means?"
The sinister seed of revenge had been planted.

Scene Four

In the midst of Paradise the object stood—test of
    true devotion, symbol of free choice. It was the tree
    of knowledge beyond innocence, beyond life.
It was the token of the freedom to love or not love—
    the "save one" of which she must not partake.

Scene Five

The rebel sought a flaw, a way to turn good to evil.
"Might I use the freedom he gave her—this capacity
    to love or not love as she chooses?
Perhaps this strength is the weakness I seek, a breach
    to exploit in my pursuit of sweet vindication.
Yes, it must be. It will be."
The villain's plot took form.

Scene Six

Donning the attire of seduction, the rebel approached
    the beloved to lure her into his bed of pleasant
    destruction.
Disguising defiance as liberation, he spoke sweet-

sounding deceptions—a titillating invitation to
rendezvous with delight.
"If you eat the fruit, you will not die but finally
know that which has been kept from you—
pleasures beyond purity, freedom from domination.
Go ahead, partake and see." Hesitant yet enticed,
the beloved reached for the bait.
A small taste. What possible harm?

Scene Seven

A chilling tremor shook eternity.
The aroma of death once again invaded the King's
domain.
Something had gone wrong, terribly wrong.
"Her choice is made, my love rejected.
Seduced by the banished rebel, no longer mine, she
accepts the deceptive caress of another. He steals
her heart to break mine.
He will rape her innocence for his sole pleasure.
He will defile her beauty and discard it as rubbish
when vengeance is complete. Oh, my beloved. My
cherished beloved!"
A tear fell down the divine cheek as his beloved
slipped willingly into the darkness.

Scene Eight

A smile of mockery formed across the rebel's mouth.
"Behold, a tear falls from the face of my enemy,
delicious fruit of the wound I have inflicted!
Only the beginning of the pain his heart will endure."
Savoring the sweet foretaste of vengeance, Lucifer
enjoyed the dawn of his heinous plot.

Scene Nine

And so it was. Freedom rejected, bondage embraced.
Divine image disfigured.
Royal destiny abandoned.
King's beloved seduced away.
Rebel's scheme crafted, tried, achieved.
No longer right. No longer good.

ACT III
DIVINE DILEMMA

Scene One

Observing his plundered prize, the rebel gloated with
hideous laughter.
"He dared force me from my rightful realm, placing
this lovely, pathetic creature in my exalted place.
Now she is mine, and he plays the fool."
In a fevered binge of impassioned rage, he began to
ravish her virgin splendor with perverse delights.

Scene Two

Intoxicated with sinister ecstasy, the rebel wiped his
mouth in momentary satisfaction, pointed toward
heaven, and declared in drunken scorn,
"If you are just, you will banish her as you banished
me!
She is guilty of the same supposed crime—rejecting
your tyrannical rule, refusing to stroke your
monstrous ego.
A bully acquires by might what he cannot otherwise
possess.
I did not bow, so you cast me out.
She does not submit, so your duty is clear."
Accusation made, the rebel resumed his sadistic
indulgence.

Scene Three

Head low, heart breaking, the King agonized over his
dilemma.
"My love must respect her choice. My justice must
punish her crime.

I can neither banish her nor draw her near.
Oh, for a remedy that will let me free my captured
  beloved."
The King's quest began—a quest to bridge the
  perilous chasm between justice and love.

Scene Four

Once pure, easily enticed by the first sensations of
  excitement, the beloved now endured the repulsive
  indulgence of prostitution.
Perfect beauty ravished away, blush of innocence
  gone, life replaced with survival.
Covering tears with laughter, she moved from one
  hollow pleasure to the next. Traveling farther down
  the path of despair, freedom forgotten, she knew
  only slavery.

Scene Five

The beloved wanted something better. Her empty,
  callous heart was stirred by brief encounters with
  enduring beauty. These faint reminders of grandeur
  and nostalgic yearnings prompted her spirit to seek
  an explanation, a purpose, a hope. Her lingering
  question: "What is my story?"

Scene Six

God spoke from beyond.
"She yearns for home but has forgotten the way.
Lost, wandering through the fog of rebel deceptions,
  she must know that I am here—that I love her, that
  I choose her still."
He sent a gift, a symbol of a pledge with her and her
  alone.

Scene Seven

The King's gift arrived—a letter describing a dignity
  long lost.
It set forth the law as an invitation back to innocence,
  charting the forgotten path. It was exacting yet
  inviting, demanding yet liberating.
Its words spoke of purpose and of hope. They told a
  story, perhaps her own.

Scene Eight

Timid, yet trusting, the beloved took a single step
  down the pathway described in the letter.
Struck by a refreshing breeze, the sweet aroma of
  pleasures past, she was compelled to take another.
The most difficult steps she had taken in some time.
The most excitement she had felt in recent memory.
Her spirit leapt in anticipation.
"Could this truly be the way home?"

Scene Nine

Leaving the path of sinister delights, the beloved
  began slipping from the rebel's firm grasp.
"The ungrateful creature wants more than the
  indulgence I provide. She dares listen to the
  Tyrant's story.
I will not allow it!"
Master of deception, lord of distraction, the rebel
  crafted a new tale to whisper in the beloved's lovely
  ear.
"You've received a letter describing a better way?
Yes, it is so. There is more to your story than you
  have seen.
Listen, and I will tell you how it may be obtained."

Scene Ten

The rebel twisted the story told in the letter, turning
love's invitation into oppressive legislation, his
captive's caring beloved into a demanding monarch.

So, accepting deeper bondage in disguise, she
abandoned her journey home to take a different
road.

Eagerly anticipating her arrival at the other end, the
King looked down the empty path and finally
returned home—alone.

Scene Eleven

And so it was.

Accusation made, enslavement complete.

Justice requiring banishment, love seeking restoration.

The beloved yearning for home, the King calling her
to freedom.

A deceptive story told, believed, embraced.

Right turned wrong. Good made evil.

ACT IV
HERO'S QUEST

Scene One

The Hero arrived in humble attire.
Peasant dwelling, modest occupation.
Capable and confident, yet meek.
The King in disguise.
He came not to conquer an empire but to win a
   heart.

Scene Two

Healing the sick, lifting the oppressed.
Feeding the hungry, raising the dead.
Instructing teachers, embracing children.
Condemning evil, forgiving sinners.
He quickly became the object of great praise—and
   envy.
Observing from a distance, the beloved's look of
   admiration betrayed her heart—she was enticed by
   his gentle strength, his impassioned purity, his kind
   eyes. Unable to part from him, she drew cautiously
   closer.

Scene Three

Her presence thrilled his heart as in days past.
He longed to reveal his identity, embrace her, and
   carry her away from the emptiness she endured.
"I dare not. She must come freely.
She must love my heart rather than fear my position."
Hand extended, he invited her to his side.
Reaching for his strong, gentle grasp, her hand
   trembled at his touch.

Their eyes met. In his, a love long forgotten.
In hers, a desperate cry for help.
The dawn of love—again.

Scene Four

The rebel reacted in hysterical rage.
"The one I most fear has come to take what is
    rightfully mine.
He seeks to steal away the lovely toy I have charmed.
I will not allow it. She belongs to me!"

Scene Five

Stirred by the Hero's words, the beloved spoke.
"I long for the love you offer.
But I dare not accept it, for I belong to another.
He gives me pleasures without joy, desire without
    satisfaction.
Yet I am indebted to him for freeing me from a
    tyrant.
My heart belongs to you, but my life to him."
Her heart was won, but the chains of bondage
    remained.
The Hero knew what must be done.

Scene Six

On a treacherous journey of rescue, the Hero
    approached the towering gates of the rebel fortress.
"I must face hate to gain love, submit to deception to
    show truth, enter darkness to reveal light."
Mindful of what he would endure, the Hero
    hesitated, wiping his brow.
"Is there no other way?"

Scene Seven

The Hero entered the enemy fortress to face his foe.
"Finally, we meet on my terms," the rebel mocked.
"How does it feel to have what you most love taken
    away?
If you are just, you will punish her betrayal by
    condemning her with me.
If you do not, you must restore my exalted post and
    bow your will to mine. Choose one—her life or
    your crown!"

Scene Eight

Resignation in his eyes, sorrow in his voice, the Hero
    spoke.
"Her betrayal must be punished. Death is the price.
It shall be dispensed in the manner you choose.
Go, make ready—your day has come."
Foretaste of victory on his lips, the rebel took leave
    to prepare.

Scene Nine

Returning to the den of captivity, the rebel drew the
    beloved close and whispered another twisted tale.
"Are you drawn to his strength, his words, his heart?
    Don't be deceived, my pretty little toy. He is not
    who he seems.
This is the Tyrant—come in disguise to punish your
    offense.
But do not fear. Listen, and I will tell you how we
    will defeat him—again." Frightened, angry,
    confused, the beloved returned to the rebel's
    comforting arms.

Scene Ten

Looming before them, a hideous instrument of
torture, suffering, and death awaited its victim. The
Hero approached the place of execution—the place
of ultimate conflict, choice, and vengeance.

Scene Eleven

The hush of silence was overtaken by the sound of
screaming.
The Hero screamed in pain from a broken body and
a breaking heart.
The rebel screamed in victory as the blood flowed
from his enemy.
The beloved screamed in sorrow as she realized
whom she had betrayed.

Scene Twelve

It was the blackest moment Creation had ever known.
Darkness had extinguished light. Death had silenced
life.
Evil had murdered good. The Hero's head hung
lifeless as a smile of gratification crossed the rebel's
face. "To the victor go the spoils," he sneered.
Wiping tears of despair, the beloved recoiled at his vile
caress.

Scene Thirteen

From the quiet of morning, the sound of shouting
erupted.
Shouts of victory, as the living Hero emerged from
death's domain.

Shouts of ruin, as the rebel saw his great triumph become his final defeat.

Shouts of hope, as the beloved's chains fell to the ground.

Scene Fourteen

Arms outstretched, the victorious King approached his trembling beloved. "Don't be afraid. The rebel has no more claim over you. Your penalty has been paid, your offense forgiven, and your life redeemed."

Eyes filled with tears of joy and regret, the beloved ran into his strong, loving embrace as he spoke the words she was longing to hear.

"Let's go home."

Scene Fifteen

Surrounded by music and dance, the King and his beloved enjoy a great feast of celebration. It is their wedding day. Every servant of the seen and unseen realms has gathered to share in a wonderful banquet of joy.

In the distance, screams of rebel madness can be faintly heard.

But none heeds as a song of jubilation ushers the King and his restored bride into the chamber of intimacy—where they will live happily ever after.

DRAMATIC REFLECTIONS

EVERY scene of the simple story you just read was derived from the teachings of Scripture, church creeds and councils, and the rich history of orthodox Christianity. It represents the main plot of Christian theology. Now we'll reflect upon the drama scene by scene in order to encounter truths that have shaped our theology but may have missed our hearts.

There are two errors we must avoid as we examine the story of God. The first is to focus purely on proposition and principle, relating to the Bible as we would an accounting textbook. In my own life, this error created a faith without passion and a life without story. The second error is to experience the enchantment of the drama without understanding the reality it portrays. This error produces a story without a punch line, a life bereft of meaning.

In this section, I seek to avoid both errors by placing drama and proposition side by side. As you read, I hope you will encounter moments of quiet inspiration, deep reflection, and startling epiphanies. I encourage you to take your time, allowing these pages to reaffirm familiar truths and awaken new dimensions to your spiritual journey. See the gospel, perhaps for the first time, through the dual lenses of proposition and plot.

ACT I

ONCE UPON A TIME

THIS story begins like any other: "Once upon a time." More precisely, once *before* time. Here we are introduced to the characters and backdrop that provide a framework for the rest of the drama.

We meet our hero; we see what his life was like before he was faced with a great quest. We encounter the villain; we discover the root of his hatred and the goal of his evil heart. We also meet a lovely, innocent creature who will become the central focus of an epic conflict between good and evil, love and hate, life and death.

ACT I Scene One
ALL IS WELL

Once upon a time God lived in perfect harmony,
   unity, and love.
Perfect harmony—for he ruled all that was.
Perfect unity—for he was the source of all truth
   and life.
Perfect love—for his very essence was so.
He was King of the universe. All was right.
   All was good.

⊕ ⊕ ⊕

The story opens with one character—God. Before anything
was, he existed: before the angelic realm, before the vast
expanse of the universe, before the dawn of time.

Have you ever wondered about his life before time began?
Of course, there's no way for us to comprehend what it's like
to exist outside the time and space continuum. We live our
lives on stage, our perspective limited by and to the scenes in
which we play our part.

Nonetheless, if we hope to understand the drama within
time and space we must realize that God is constrained by
neither. God exists both on- and offstage; he is the central
character of history, but he also views the entire spectrum of
creation and time from outside, beyond, above. All that
exists within the spiritual and physical realms originated
with him. All that is good reflects his nature. All that is evil
rejects it.

*In the beginning was the Word, and the Word was with God, and the
Word was God. He was with God in the beginning. (John 1:1-2)*

47

The Word was not just an idea or a life force. The Word was a person. Not an *it* but a *he.* He is more of a person than you or I. All those good things that define our personalities reflect his own. When we laugh or cry, we reflect his emotions. When we create, we reflect his creativity. When we love, we reflect his heart. We are persons only because he is a person.

As the ruler and source of everything good, his life must have been filled with many good things before the created order as we know it existed. We know that there was perfect harmony because nothing existed that was inconsistent with his nature. Perfect unity reigned because the Father, Son, and Spirit are one in eternal intimacy. He enjoyed perfect love because that's his nature. But I imagine he also enjoyed a good piece of music, a funny joke, a beautiful painting, and an exciting story. I'm sure he liked to invent new gadgets in his workshop.

After all, our existence was his idea and his doing.

ACT I Scene Two
DIVINE ARTIST

God expressed himself through boundless creativity:
Painting beautiful scenes on the canvas of eternity.
Composing thrilling symphonies for the universe to
   perform.
Engineering a perfectly ordered cosmos.
Scripting epic dramas for the stage of life.
The divine artist at work in his gallery, every creation
   an expression of his passionate heart.

⊕ ⊕ ⊕

God's heart has always been filled with passion. That passion is experienced and expressed through beauty, music, adventure, romance, drama, humor, imagination, science, mathematics, language, art, and the countless other inventions originating in his workshop. The order and wonders of our world reveal his intellect and creativity. Who he is can be known by observing what he has made.

> *For since the creation of the world God's invisible qualities—his eternal power and divine nature—have been clearly seen, being understood from what has been made. (Romans 1:20)*

God the artist created something out of nothing. He composed the symphony others merely echo, painted the masterpiece others reflect, wrote the story others try to tell. He engineered the first architectural structures, called mountains and trees; programmed the first computer, called a brain; and invented the first miracle drug, called the immune system. They all started in his imagination—an imagination that has inspired our own.

Think of it. Every piece of music composed by Beethoven or the Beatles started as a tune in his head. Every painting of Michelangelo's is a copy of something hanging on his refrigerator door. Every one of Thomas Edison's inventions started as a concept on the back of his napkin. The stuff of every Shakespearean play, Einstein discovery, Disney film, and Microsoft upgrade originated in the mind of God. We compose, paint, invent, write, and plan only because he did it first.

He is before all things, and in him all things hold together.
(Colossians 1:17)

In his stirring book *Windows of the Soul,* author Ken Gire
suggests that we create because we are hoping to connect with
our Creator.

We painted to see if what was lost was in the picture. We composed to
hear if what was lost was in the music. We sculpted to find if what
was lost was in the stone. We wrote to discover if what was lost was
in the story. . . . We reach for God in many ways. Through our
sculptures and our scriptures. Through our pictures and our prayers.
Through our writing and our worship. And through them He reaches
for us. . . . His search begins with something said. Ours begins with
something heard. His begins with something shown. Ours, with
something seen. (Gire, 16-17)

What we see, what we hear, what we know all came to be
because God, the central character in our story, expressed the
passions of his heart. The grand history of human invention,
creation, and discovery are our efforts to know him, to touch
him on a deeper level—a level that can only be reached by
following in his footsteps.

ACT I *Scene Three*
ROYAL DOMAIN

This good King built a spectacular city.
Its citizens were a host of servants—those to whom
   he had given the gift of life. He appointed leaders
   to direct his affairs and entrusted them with the

capacity and authority necessary to rule throughout his domain.

Governed under the firm yet loving rule of the King, all citizens of this great city lived with an enduring sense of wonder, reverence, and peace.

⊕ ⊕ ⊕

Heaven. Angels. The unseen realities of the spiritual realm. They existed before the material world. They are part of the stage and cast contributing to a drama that began long before any of us entered the picture. The unseen is every bit as real as the seen. God made them both.

For by him all things were created: things in heaven and on earth, visible and invisible, whether thrones or powers or rulers or authorities; all things were created by him and for him. (Colossians 1:16)

Like the microscopic universe comprised of protons, neutrons, atoms, and energy, there are concrete realities that we can neither see nor exist without. With an ironic twist, God made the invisible world as the context within which the visible world exists. So what we can't see is the context within which what we can see is understood. And if the material universe is merely a reflection of the true royal domain, what a sight the unseen must be!

On a few occasions, men have been allowed to catch a tiny glimpse of the spiritual realm.

• They've seen a King on his throne.

Your throne, O God, will last for ever and ever; a scepter of justice will be the scepter of your kingdom. (Psalm 45:6)

The Lord is in his holy temple; the Lord is on his heavenly throne.
(Psalm 11:4)

• They've seen a brilliant city.

He carried me away in the Spirit to a mountain great and high, and
showed me the Holy City, Jerusalem, coming down out of heaven
from God. It shone with the glory of God, and its brilliance was
like that of a very precious jewel, like a jasper, clear as crystal.
(Revelation 21:10-11)

• They've seen servants.

I saw the Lord sitting on his throne with all the host of
heaven standing around him on his right and on his left.
(1 Kings 22:19)

God established a domain that includes millions of angelic
beings in an organized hierarchy who are given specific
assignments to fulfill his purposes (Revelation 5:11, Ephesians 3:10, Jude 1:9, Luke 1:26).

His majesty their object of awe and source of wonder,
God's servants join his created order shouting the preemi-
nent unseen reality, "Holy, holy, holy, is the Lord
Almighty"(Isaiah 6:3).

ACT I *Scene Four*
TRUSTED SERVANT

There was a leader among the King's host who was
exalted above all others, as the King had ordained
him to be. Lucifer was a model of perfection, full

of wisdom and beauty—for the King had made him so.

He was the King's most trusted servant, appointed guardian over the King's most cherished domain—that place reserved for his greatest work of love.

⊕ ⊕ ⊕

King Arthur had Lancelot. The Lone Ranger had Tonto. Batman had Robin. Serving every great hero are loyal followers. Usually one rises above all others, entrusted with the most prosperous region, the most confidential secret, the most critical mission. In the divine drama that one was the highest-ranking archangel, named Lucifer.

Set aside for the moment any images you may have of Lucifer. At this point in the story, he is untainted by the events described in subsequent scenes. He is the perfect right-hand man, confidant, and loyal servant. Lucifer is bright, articulate, and adorned with splendid beauty. He has it all. In a passage most scholars agree is describing Lucifer, Ezekiel gives us a snapshot of what he was like while serving God.

You were the model of perfection, full of wisdom and perfect in beauty. You were in Eden, the garden of God; every precious stone adorned you: ruby, topaz and emerald, chrysolite, onyx and jasper, sapphire, turquoise and beryl. Your settings and mountings were made of gold; on the day you were created they were prepared. (Ezekiel 28:12-13)

Ezekiel also records God's words to Lucifer concerning the position Lucifer held in God's domain.

You were anointed as a guardian cherub, for so I ordained you. You were on the holy mount of God; you walked among the fiery stones. (Ezekiel 28:14)

Lucifer was ordained by God to serve in his inner circle as "guardian cherub" over "Eden, the garden of God." The precise meaning of this term is uncertain, but it seems to represent an honored post only worthy of the most trusted servant. We know Eden as the place God would perform his greatest work of creation. It's doubtful that any domain was as near and dear to God's heart. So, like any wise ruler, he placed it under the protection and jurisdiction of his most talented and gifted steward, Lucifer. And for a time, Lucifer executed that responsibility flawlessly.

You were blameless in your ways from the day you were created. (Ezekiel 28:15)

But one day, for some reason, everything changed.

ACT I *Scene Five*
THE BIRTH OF DEATH

Filled with the insanity of pride, he who had been
given most turned against the giver. No longer
content to worship the King, Lucifer incited
rebellion. "Why must there be only one God? Why
must all bow to him alone? I will no longer serve,
but rule. I will no longer submit my will. Yes, I will
be like the Most High!"
Persuading many he governed to join him, he
declared war.

It was a minor skirmish put down by the King's
might, but it was a betrayal that pierced his heart.
Demanding separation from the source of life,
Lucifer gave birth to death.

⊕ ⊕ ⊕

Every story requires a villain. David confronted Goliath.
Peter Pan battled Captain Hook. Luke Skywalker faced
Darth Vader. It's the conflict between good and evil, hero
and villain, that creates the drama. Without conflict, there
can be no quest, risk, victory, or intrigue. In our story, the
villain is a once-trusted servant turned betrayer. He who was
given most used it to incite rebellion.

Why do those given much demand more? Why do those who
should be grateful instead resent the giver? It makes little sense.
Nonetheless, it's the pattern of a folly called pride. A folly that
was born in the heart of God's most trusted servant, Lucifer.

*You were blameless in your ways from the day you were created till
wickedness was found in you. Through your widespread trade you
were filled with violence, and you sinned. . . . Your heart became
proud on account of your beauty, and you corrupted your wisdom
because of your splendor. (Ezekiel 28:15-17)*

Dig below the surface of all evil and you will find that the root
is pride. It is pride that demands its way, refuses to submit,
rebels against authority, and inflates its own sense of worth
beyond sanity. And it is pride that drives the created one to
shake his fist in the face of his Creator and demand the throne.

*You said in your heart, "I will ascend to heaven; I will raise my
throne above the stars of God; I will sit enthroned on the mount of*

assembly, on the utmost heights of the sacred mountain. I will ascend above the tops of the clouds; I will make myself like the Most High."
(Isaiah 14:13-14)

This is the insanity of pride. One who was spoken into existence by God saw himself as God's equal. Unwilling to remain an honored servant, Lucifer made his play for the top role. A noble war against an arrogant tyrant, or a delusional boycott of reality? Mad as a mouse declaring himself to be a lion. Foolish as a tree cutting itself off from its life-sustaining roots. The folly of pride drove Lucifer too far.

Death is the opposite of life. It's not the end of existence but the beginning of something far worse—an eternity of madness and deception, separated from the source of sanity and truth.

Demanding the freedom to control his own destiny, Lucifer became a slave to his own hatred. Jesus said that he who wishes to find his life must lose it. Lucifer got it backwards. And thus, death was born.

ACT I *Scene Six*
BANISHED

> Victim of his own folly, architect of his own fall, the traitor was banished from the King's court—moving from friend to foe, from love to hate, from servant to saboteur, from honor to shame.
> Eager to strike back, he nurtured the bitter seed of vengeance within his darkened heart. "My day will come!"

⊕ ⊕ ⊕

Banished. Thrown out. Defeated. Punished. Dishonored. Call it what you will. The once-exalted servant named Lucifer became a disgraced outcast known as Satan, Beelzebub, Serpent, and the devil.

> *I drove you in disgrace from the mount of God, and I expelled you, O guardian cherub, from among the fiery stones. (Ezekiel 28:16)*
>
> *I threw you to the earth; I made a spectacle of you. (Ezekiel 28:17)*
>
> *You are brought down to the grave, to the depths of the pit. (Isaiah 14:15)*

But Satan neither accepted his defeat nor submitted to the reality that was, is, and will always be—"The Lord is one" (Deuteronomy 6:4). Clinging to the illusion that one day he would possess or destroy the throne of God, Satan became the villain who inspires all other villains.

No bad guy has ever matched his cunning or determination. Establishing the despicable standard every trickster, liar, and cheat seeks to achieve, Satan was the champion of the historical Goliath's blasphemy and the inspiration for the fictional Captain Hook's twisted paranoia.

It is vital that we understand this subplot if we hope to make sense of the divine drama. Those who reject the reality of Satan, considering themselves "enlightened beyond such superstition," are tearing crucial pages out of the script. As we will discover, much of the drama, and of life, hinges upon facing the hard reality that there is an evil heart set upon vengeance in our world. It's the twist behind many turns, the motivation of many characters, and the context within which our part of the story begins.

ACT I Scene Seven
RISK

The bitter aftertaste of betrayal lingering still, the
  King spoke.
"I desire one to love beyond all others, one to shower
  with my favor, one with whom I can share my
  heart."
Though surrounded by servants, the King yearned for
  a bride.
One who would not be obliged to serve his position
  but free to respond to his heart. Risking another
  betrayal, the King sought a true love.

⊕ ⊕ ⊕

Musicians compose. Artists paint. Dancers dance. Writers
write. They don't act in order to become. They act because
they already are. If you want to understand who a person is,
watch what he or she does.

Giving us the gift of life was more than an act of inspiration or passion. It was an expression of who God is—something he could not talk himself out of doing. Even though it
would have been far less of a hassle to maintain the status
quo, God took an enormous risk. Why would the one who
needs no one want a lover? Why would he set himself up for
the possibility of heartache and pain?

Each Christmas season my family and I enjoy watching a
holiday special called *The Homecoming*. Set during the Great
Depression, this film inspired a weekly television series about
the Walton family. Throughout the story, young John-Boy
Walton finds himself unable to contain his passion for writing. Periodically retrieving a hidden paper tablet, John-Boy

feverishly writes down the ideas and thoughts trapped inside his head that scream to be expressed on the page. Though too embarrassed by his compulsion to tell anyone, he can't stop. As he finally admits to his concerned mother, he feels as if he will go crazy if he doesn't write. John-Boy is a writer. He has to write.

God is love. Therefore, he has to love. He can no more keep this love to himself than John-Boy could keep his ideas off the tablet page. It was a deep yearning to express his love—to share his heart with another person—that drove God to create mankind. He didn't make us so that we would love him but so that he could love us. We were not made to be a race of servants but to be the object of God's affection.

This is love: not that we loved God, but that he loved us. (1 John 4:10)

God is a lover who wants a true love. That's why you and I exist.

ACT I *Scene Eight*
BELOVED

Love breathed new life—life unlike all others.
He created a masterpiece after his own image, one
   who was more than mere servant. She was made to
   be the supreme object of the King's affection.
Made to be loved, free to love in return—or not to
   love.
A living portrait of his own nature, God's cherished
   beloved.

⊕ ⊕ ⊕

The closest we can come to understanding how God must have felt during this moment in the drama is to look at its faint reflection in other stories: the moment Romeo's heart skips a beat upon meeting the lovely Juliet, the day Captain Georg von Trapp finds himself inexplicably attracted to Maria in *The Sound of Music*, the second Tom Hanks spots Meg Ryan in the airport and later atop the Empire State Building in *Sleepless in Seattle*, that first nervous date when I fell madly in love with the woman I have now been married to since 1985.

These and other scenes reflect a moment in the divine drama when everything changed for our hero.

So God created man in his own image, in the image of God he created him; male and female he created them. (Genesis 1:27)

The Lord God formed the man from the dust of the ground and breathed into his nostrils the breath of life, and the man became a living being. (Genesis 2:7)

Many of us have read and reread the biblical account of the creation of mankind to the point that it's become quite familiar. Perhaps too familiar. We have such limited comprehension of what was taking place at the moment Adam took his first breath.

This was perhaps the most thrilling moment in all eternity for God. After all, he was not just making another creature. He was meeting his future bride.

I wonder if his heart skipped a beat.

I bet he couldn't take his eyes off of the beauty of his beloved.

Perhaps he was a little nervous.

Who knows what went through the mind of God at the moment his beloved entered his life? One thing is certain: nothing would ever be the same again!

ACT I Scene Nine
TOGETHER

> Overflowing with excitement, the divine lover
>   proclaimed the passion of his heart.
> "How I love her! She is priceless to me, precious
>   beyond words. My heart leaps as we walk in the
>   cool of the day. I ache for her to know my heart. I
>   made her to be loved and to love freely in return.
>   For with freedom comes pure devotion. She will
>   not be obliged but willingly drawn. Oh, how I love
>   those moments when hand in hand we share the
>   thrilling oneness of intimate hearts."

⊕ ⊕ ⊕

Have you ever had a crush on someone? There's nothing quite so wonderful and awful. The thrill of their presence—even their voice. You notice everything—how she dresses, how he walks. The upward or downward curve of an eyebrow can make or break your week. Being anxious over the uncertainty, hoping he or she will notice you—perhaps even like you, and maybe someday love you. Remember getting tongue-tied in the middle of an ordinary conversation about some insignificant topic? You so wanted to make a good impression that you made a fool of yourself. At least that's the way it felt.

I think this is a bit of what it was like for God during those first days with Adam and Eve. Unlike God, most of our nervousness is tied to insecurity. But there is also an element of uncertainty in courtship that both inspires and threatens the joy of new love. God created mankind with a free will, able to accept or reject his affection. God loved them more than a new mother loves her infant, more than a newlywed loves his bride. He knew everything there was to know about them, more than they knew themselves. But he could not, would not, come on too strong. He wanted an intimacy that only occurs when both parties choose it. They could not be forced, compelled, or manipulated into such a love. They had to be drawn.

Can you imagine what it must have been like for Adam and Eve? Everything was new to them. They were like newborn babes trying to understand their surroundings but with full capacity for understanding all they encountered. It had to be overwhelming and exhilarating! Basking in the tender care of their Creator, walking hand in hand with him "in the cool of the day" (Genesis 3:8) and enjoying the sights, sounds, smells, and tastes of a virgin world. God and his beloved were like a couple on their first date—each discovering just how wonderful the other could be.

ACT I *Scene Ten*
PARADISE

The King gave his beloved a perfectly prepared home, enfolding his cherished with spectacular beauty. He showered her with gifts from his heart, placing her in a garden filled with all that is good.

Every day was filled with the wonder of discovery
and the thrill of adventure, every moment warmed
by the haven of acceptance.
It was a place to walk and talk together, a place to
call home.
Paradise.

⊕ ⊕ ⊕

Eden. A place of beauty. A place of innocence. A place unlike any we can comprehend—perfectly designed for its inhabitants to enjoy the most satisfying, healthy, adventurous, and pleasure-filled lives possible. I wonder if it had the sandy beaches of a tropical paradise. Did it have the breathtaking majesty of the Rocky Mountains, the crashing waves of the Oregon coast, the fresh breeze of an eastern seaport, or the sweet aroma of a Midwestern apple farm? More than likely, it had them all—and more.

The Bible describes Eden as a garden entrusted to Adam's care and dominion. From this we know it was a place of beauty.

Now the Lord God had planted a garden in the east, in Eden; and there he put the man he had formed. And the Lord God made all kinds of trees grow out of the ground—trees that were pleasing to the eye and good for food. In the middle of the garden were the tree of life and the tree of the knowledge of good and evil. A river watering the garden flowed from Eden; from there it was separated into four headwaters. . . . The Lord God took the man and put him in the Garden of Eden to work it and take care of it. (Genesis 2:8-10, 15)

We also know that Eden was a place of innocence. Adam and

Eve were free of the self-conscious insecurities that dominate our lives today.

> *The man and his wife were both naked, and they felt no shame.*
> *(Genesis 2:25)*

At this point in human history, everything in existence was good, a gift from the heart and hand of a good God. Adam, Eve, and their descendants had so much to look forward to. From tasting their first mixed-fruit drink to orbiting earth in a space shuttle—a whole world of discovery, invention, and adventure was waiting to be enjoyed. All of it a gift from God, their passionate suitor.

ACT I Scene Eleven
MADE RIGHT

> And so it was. Magnificent creativity achieved.
> Royal domain established.
> Rebellion thwarted. Rebel banished.
> The King's beloved basking in his tender care.
> All was made right. All was made good.

⊕ ⊕ ⊕

And so the curtain closes on the first act of our story.

We have met the central character—catching a glimpse of his passion, his majesty, his creativity, and, most importantly, his heart.

We have seen the rebellion of a once-trusted and exalted servant and his desire for revenge.

We have learned that God, in pursuit of true love, has made one with whom he intends to divulge his heart and share his domain.

A world of wonderful discovery, adventure, and beauty lay before an innocent beloved.

So it was, "Once upon a time."

ACT II

VILLAIN'S PLOT

THE second act of our drama centers on Lucifer's obsession with—and blueprint for—revenge. As with all things evil, we see his diabolical brilliance for twisting truth into lies, purity into perversity, and life into death. We gain a deeper understanding of why God made mankind and just how pivotal the events described in the third chapter of Genesis are to the divine drama of human history.

ACT II Scene One
BITTER AFFLICTION

In the depths of darkness, the rebel endured the
   shame of bitter affliction. From the heart of hatred
   he spoke to a legion of wavering loyalists, seeking
   to inspire the hope of regaining what had been lost.
"We are not defeated; the war has only just begun.
   Better to reign in hell than serve in heaven! No
   longer bound by the dictates of the Tyrant, we are
   free to live in a world of our own making. We are
   gods—rulers of our own destiny, liberators of all
   who seek to be as they will rather than as he wills.
   Doubt not, our day will come!"
The empty ravings of madness in desperate search for
   an occasion to avenge his shame.

⊕ ⊕ ⊕

In the year 1663 English poet John Milton completed his
five-year effort to write what is considered one of the greatest achievements in English literature. His epic poem entitled *Paradise Lost* was intended, in Milton's words, to "assert
Eternal Providence, and justify the ways of God to men"
(I.25-26). A central theme of this masterpiece is the rebellion of Lucifer and his effort to undermine God's plan for
mankind.

In what has become one of the most famous passages of
this epic work, Milton paints a picture of what it must have
been like among the fallen angelic beings who had joined
Lucifer's failed coup attempt, only to find themselves cast

into hell along with their leader. In an effort to comfort them with the hope of yet regaining heaven, Lucifer raises his fist to God's throne and declares of hell,

> *Here we may reign secure, and in my choice*
> *To reign is worth ambition though in Hell:*
> *Better to reign in Hell, than serve in Heav'n. (1.261-263)*

So profoundly twisted was his heart after the rebellion, Lucifer dedicated his entire existence to thwarting God's purposes and plans. He commissioned his fallen host to the task of undermining the God-designed goodness with the evil that is its absence.

> *Fall'n Cherub, to be weak is miserable Doing or Suffering: but*
> *of this be sure,*
> *To do aught good never will be our task, But ever to do ill our sole*
> *delight,*
> *As being the contrary to his high will Whom we resist. If then*
> *his Providence*
> *Out of our evil seek to bring forth good, Our labour must be to*
> *pervert that end,*
> *And out of good still to find means of evil. (1.156-165)*

I have often wondered what could possibly keep Satan motivated in light of his obvious inability to defeat the supreme power of almighty God. Milton finds the answer in Lucifer's belief that he will one day win. But as we'll discover, he doesn't intend to win through superior force. Rather, Satan intends to win by using God's own love and goodness as weapons against him so that he might "out of good still ... find means of evil."

ACT II *Scene Two*
DOMINION

The King glanced at his beloved—more beautiful
than ever with the light of his gaze resting upon
her. Approaching softly with an unguarded heart,
he directed her attention to the magnificent works
around them—the regal strength of a mountain
range, the breathtaking luster of the setting sun,
and the gentle symphony of a breeze-blown forest.
"I made these for you. They are the expression of my
being. I crafted them before you were formed. I've
shared them with no other. Enjoy them. Each is a
symbol of my abiding affection. They are all
yours—save one." Receiving his gifts, she was
stirred by his majestic splendor and touched by his
tender heart.

⊕ ⊕ ⊕

Back in the Garden of Eden, unaware of the rebellion occur-
ring in the unseen realm, Adam and Eve were enjoying the
good gifts of God—including delicious foods and juices, a
wildlife park filled with purebred animals of every sort, beautiful scenery, and perfect weather. All of these creations were
placed under Adam and Eve's domain.

"Rule over the fish of the sea and the birds of the air and over every
living creature that moves on the ground." Then God said, "I give you
every seed-bearing plant on the face of the whole earth and every tree
that has fruit with seed in it. They will be yours for food. And to all
the beasts of the earth and all the birds of the air and all the creatures
that move on the ground—everything that has the breath of life in

it—I give every green plant for food." And it was so.
(Genesis 1:28-30)

God also gave them the gift of pure and passionate sexual intimacy. In fact, he commanded them to experience the kind of love between a husband and wife that produces children when he said,

Be fruitful and increase in number; fill the earth and subdue it.
(Genesis 1:28)

God never intended for man to serve Creation but to rule over and protect it. He never intended sex to be a source of guilt and heartache but an expression of passion and purity. That's how it was in Eden.

What a contrast! Lucifer was created best and brightest among the unseen host, just as Adam and Eve were in the seen world. Lucifer had been entrusted with the best domain in the unseen realm. Adam and Eve were given authority over every living creation on earth. Both were God's representatives. But in this instance, dominion was given as a gift to be enjoyed. It was an expression of God's love for the one he cherished—a love he yearned for his beloved to accept. It was a love that drew her to him, but a love she had the freedom to reject.

ACT II Scene Three
SINISTER SEED

From the throne of evil came a leap of devilish delight. "What fortune! My opportunity for vengeance has arrived.

The Tyrant has foolishly given his heart to another.
Though I cannot defeat his might, perhaps I can
   subvert his love.
But by what means? By what means?"
The sinister seed of revenge had been planted.

⊕ ⊕ ⊕

No matter how powerful, brave, or noble a hero may be, he becomes vulnerable to defeat when he loves another. A window of opportunity opens for an unscrupulous enemy to gain the edge, for a cowardly foe's manipulation to gain unfair advantage in the battle.

Capture his child and threaten harm if demands aren't met.

Rape his bride and turn him into a madman driven by rage rather than a warrior disciplined by calculated strategy.

Or better yet, steal away the affection of the one he seeks to save, undermining his resolve by turning the quest into a pointless pursuit.

Through one means or another, the object of a hero's love can become the key to a villain's victory. Lucifer, the mastermind behind all diabolical brilliance, invented the strategy. As soon as God gave his heart to another, Satan began seeking his opportunity to use it for his advantage.

In the movie *Hook*, Robin Williams plays the now-adult Peter Pan, who has a successful career, a lovely wife, and two young children. Through a series of events, Peter finds himself back in Neverland facing his old foe Captain Hook, who has kidnapped his kids in hopes of luring Peter into battle. It works. Peter attempts to rescue his children from the evil clutches of Hook. But then, thanks to the deceptive manipulation of Hook, Peter's oldest boy, Jack, turns on his father. Unaware that he is being used as a pawn for Hook's

revenge, Jack becomes attached to Captain Hook, preferring the irresponsible indulgence Hook allows to the strict
responsibility mandated by his real dad. Peter's heart is
broken and focus lost when he observes Jack and Hook
together in a father-and-son type relationship. Jack no
longer wants his father to save him. In the diabolical spirit
of Lucifer, Hook used the one Peter loved and hoped to
save as a tool to gain the advantage. Knowing he would lose
a fair fight, Hook raised the stakes by changing the nature
of the conflict.

Lucifer was no fool. It was clear that he lacked the strength
to challenge God's vastly superior might. So he plotted to
change the nature of the conflict. That was his strategy. All he
needed then was the opportunity.

ACT II *Scene Four*
SAVE ONE

In the midst of Paradise the object stood—test of
    true devotion, symbol of free choice. It was the tree
    of knowledge beyond innocence, beyond life.
It was the token of the freedom to love or not love—
    the "save one" of which she must not partake.

⊕ ⊕ ⊕

Imagine everything you could ever want being placed before
you with the invitation to enjoy it all. You may partake as
much, as often, and as long as you like. No limits. No guilt.
No calories. The only concession on your part is to stay away
from one tree with a particular type of fruit. Anything and

everything in the world in exchange for one restriction. Who wouldn't jump at such a deal? Adam and Eve were given the chance.

> *And the Lord God commanded the man, "You are free to eat from any tree in the garden; but you must not eat from the tree of the knowledge of good and evil, for when you eat of it you will surely die." (Genesis 2:16-17)*

Why would God place something in the Garden that he didn't want Adam or Eve to experience? If Eden was a gift to be enjoyed and managed by them, why include something that might be harmful? It isn't as if God had to include the tree. Couldn't he just have left it out of the Garden to avoid problems?

God made mankind to be his beloved—someone with whom he could have a mutually chosen relationship. The tree was a symbol of Adam and Eve's freedom to accept or reject God's offer of intimacy. The tree was placed in the Garden not to tempt but to testify. It stood as a symbol, a daily reminder to Adam and Eve that they could enjoy God's loving protection or chart their own course. The choice was made clear and the consequences explained. It wasn't necessarily the fruit from the tree that was harmful but what it represented.

Had there been no tree, there would have been no choice. Had there been no freedom to choose, there could have been no real love. In the words of Milton's *Paradise Lost,* Adam and Eve were:

> *Sufficient to have stood, though free to fall. . . .*
> *Not free, what proof could they have giv'n sincere,*
> *Of true allegiance, Constant Faith or Love? (3.99,103-104)*

Adam and Eve, our representatives, were given a choice that would determine the course of all human history (I Corinthians 15:22). That choice was made each time they walked past the fruit hanging from a tree that could give knowledge beyond innocence and experiences beyond the rich adventure life was made to be.

ACT II *Scene Five*
FATAL FLAW

> The rebel sought a flaw, a way to turn good to evil.
> "Might I use the freedom he gave her—this capacity
>   to love or not love as she chooses?
> Perhaps this strength is the weakness I seek, a breach
>   to exploit in my pursuit of sweet vindication.
> Yes, it must be. It will be."
> The villain's plot took form.

⊕ ⊕ ⊕

Lucifer's opportunity had come. He would use something good as a tool for ill. Evil is unable to create anything original. It is only able to twist and pervert that which God has created through downward innovation. As darkness is the absence of light and wrong the opposite of right, so choice could open the door to slavery. A wrong choice can rob the chooser of true freedom. Passionate love could be twisted into empty indulgence by changing its object from another to the self. God could be changed from lover to oppressor by making the tree a sign of deprivation rather than a symbol of affection.

What is true freedom? To many, inspired by Lucifer's rebellion, true freedom is rejecting all forms of authority—being master of one's own destiny, god of one's own life. But there is a catch. With rejection of God-ordained authority comes slavery to one's own passions and limitations. No longer able to choose good, a person with such "freedom" is left with nothing but the marred scraps of evil.

True freedom is the ability to choose, from the countless good gifts of God, that which he created for us to experience without guilt or consequence. Unspoiled by rebellion against true beauty and goodness, we're free to enjoy pleasures made for deep fulfillment rather than empty enslavement.

Lucifer's plot was a stroke of diabolical brilliance. By changing the good of freedom into the evil of slavery, he could steal away the heart of one in order to break the heart of another.

ACT II *Scene Six*
APPLE CONSPIRACY

Donning the attire of seduction, the rebel approached
   the beloved to lure her into his bed of pleasant
   destruction.
Disguising defiance as liberation, he spoke sweet-
   sounding deceptions—a titillating invitation to
   rendezvous with delight.
"If you eat the fruit, you will not die but finally
   know that which has been kept from you—
   pleasures beyond purity, freedom from domination.
   Go ahead, partake and see." Hesitant yet enticed,
   the beloved reached for the bait.
A small taste. What possible harm?

⊕ ⊕ ⊕

As the drama unfolds, this is a defining scene. It is the moment when the plots of the seen and the unseen worlds collide. The once-trusted servant turned rebel enters time and space to approach God's innocent beloved. Wrapped in the form of the most mysterious creature in the garden and drawing upon the faint echo of beauty residing within his otherwise corrupt existence, Satan seduces the beloved with sweet-sounding deceptions.

A fulfilled, cherished bride who trusts her husband cannot be seduced away. But if something causes her to feel neglected or unappreciated, she becomes more vulnerable. Add the suggestion that her trust has been violated, and she begins to feel she has reason to seek comfort in the arms of another. Lucifer had to cause Adam and Eve to question the affection and trustworthiness of their God. Twisting truth into a question, he very intentionally plants the idea that God's true desire was to withhold more from them than they realized.

Now the serpent was more crafty than any of the wild animals the Lord God had made. He said to the woman, "Did God really say, 'You must not eat from any tree in the garden'?" (Genesis 3:1)

"*Any* tree in the garden?" he says. But God had placed a restriction on only one tree. In fact, he clearly said they could eat of every other tree. Did Lucifer misspeak? Not at all. Read between the lines and discover his true intent: "One restriction is only the beginning. Why any restrictions at all? I'll tell you why! He's withholding more than you know. He's keeping you from your true destiny. Threatened by anyone who invades his domain of arrogance, he wants you to remain inferior in order to stroke his monstrous ego."

Responding to Eve's attempt to clarify the command, Lucifer paints God as one with less-than-noble intentions, one who may be less than trustworthy.

"You will not surely die," the serpent said to the woman. "For God knows that when you eat of it your eyes will be opened, and you will be like God, knowing good and evil." (Genesis 3:4-5)

At this moment two powerful forces converge: pleasure and deception. The first, a good created by God. The second, an evil conspired by Satan.

When the woman saw that the fruit of the tree was good for food and pleasing to the eye, and also desirable for gaining wisdom, she took some and ate it. She also gave some to her husband, who was with her, and he ate it. (Genesis 3:6)

It was good for food. It was pleasing to the eye. It would give wisdom. What could God have against such things? Perhaps he really was threatened, driven by arrogance, unworthy of their love.

Shaken by a lie and driven by desire, the beloved enters the embrace of another: God's enemy—and her own.

ACT II *Scene Seven*
ETERNAL TREMOR

A chilling tremor shook eternity.
The aroma of death once again invaded the King's domain.
Something had gone wrong, terribly wrong.

"Her choice is made, my love rejected.
Seduced by the banished rebel, no longer mine, she
    accepts the deceptive caress of another. He steals
    her heart to break mine.
He will rape her innocence for his sole pleasure.
He will defile her beauty and discard it as rubbish
    when vengeance is complete. Oh, my beloved. My
    cherished beloved!"
A tear fell down the divine cheek as his beloved
    slipped willingly into the darkness.

⊕ ⊕ ⊕

Learning that your youngest child is dying of cancer. Discovering your spouse in bed with another lover. Helplessly watching as your teen sacrifices her innocence on the altar of rebellion. Being falsely accused of a crime you didn't commit—by your best friend. The agonizing pain of these tragic events combined to create the greatest heartbreak ever known. God felt them all, and more, during the eternal tremor of the Fall.

Then the eyes of both of them were opened, and they realized they were naked; so they sewed fig leaves together and made coverings for themselves. Then the man and his wife heard the sound of the Lord God as he was walking in the garden in the cool of the day, and they hid from the Lord God among the trees of the garden. But the Lord God called to the man, "Where are you?" (Genesis 3:7-9)

"Where are you?" Three terrible words that said it all. The days of walking hand in hand during the cool of the day, of intimate oneness, had ended. The pain of death and the heartache of separation had begun. I believe God wept from the knowledge of what his beloved would endure at the hands of his enemy. He grieved over the stench of impurity and the mire of wickedness mankind would willingly embrace. Already sinking into the dark quicksand of sin's control, Adam and Eve admit several previously unknown feelings— fear, shame, and a desire to hide themselves.

> *"I heard you in the garden, and I was afraid because I was naked; so I hid." And [God] said, "Who told you that you were naked? Have you eaten from the tree that I commanded you not to eat from?" (Genesis 3:10-11)*

Sinking further still, they blame others for their own willing choice.

> *The man said, "The woman you put here with me—she gave me some fruit from the tree, and I ate it." (Genesis 3:12)*

> *The woman said, "The serpent deceived me, and I ate." (Genesis 3:13)*

Knowledge beyond purity had come, and there was no turning back. The reality of life apart from God was now theirs, and it was a cold, dark, and barren place. Like the rebel who had lured them into his domain, Adam and Eve got what they craved. Whether or not they would like it was another matter.

ACT II *Scene Eight*
VINDICATION

A smile of mockery formed across the rebel's mouth.
"Behold, a tear falls from the face of my enemy,
delicious fruit of the wound I have inflicted!

Only the beginning of the pain his heart will endure."
Savoring the sweet foretaste of vengeance, Lucifer
enjoyed the dawn of his heinous plot.

⊕ ⊕ ⊕

We rarely consider what the Fall meant in the unseen realm. We focus instead upon the bad things introduced into the human experience, such as sickness, pain, death, and sorrow. But what did it mean to the other two characters in our drama?

First, for Satan, this was his moment. Finally able to strike back for the humiliation he had experienced after his failed uprising, Lucifer reveled in his victory over the one he saw as an arrogant Tyrant. Crazed with the madness of self-deception, Satan had been frustrated for some time with his inability to strike back. Too weak for a direct attack, yet too strong to accept his defeat, Satan knew this was the perfect means of vengeance.

For God, it was like a knife through the heart. All at once, he lost that which had been so perfect. The wonderful honeymoon of intimacy between God and mankind was destroyed as the bride was found in bed with another lover. I wonder whether at that moment God regretted giving us a free will. Did he consider taking it back? Did he weep at the knowledge of the horrors we would experience in days to come? Did he wish he could protect us from our own folly by erasing the consequences of sin? Of course he did. But he couldn't. Not because he wasn't powerful enough, but because he refuses to force himself on anyone or push his way into our lives. When we chose to reject the good that he is, we embraced all of the bad that he isn't. We embraced a reality that, more than anything else, must have been the cause of tremendous grief.

In the unseen realm, Satan laughed while God wept.

ACT II *Scene Nine*
WOUND

> And so it was. Freedom rejected, bondage embraced.
> Divine image disfigured.
> Royal destiny abandoned.
> King's beloved seduced away.
> Rebel's scheme crafted, tried, achieved.
> No longer right. No longer good.

⊕ ⊕ ⊕

As we end Act II, the villain has the upper hand.

Our central character's love has been spurned, his offer rejected, and his heart broken.

Mankind, God's beloved, has entered the arms of another, one who seems exciting and trustworthy. She doesn't realize that he seeks to use her for his own pleasure and as a pawn in his quest for revenge.

Lucifer has managed to strike back like an incensed snake. By seducing away God's true love, he seems to have gained an unfair advantage, exploiting God's one vulnerability.

A wound has been inflicted, setting the stage for Act III.

ACT III

DIVINE DILEMMA

IN ACT III, the stakes have been raised in the great conflict between God and Lucifer. Having successfully stabbed his enemy, the rebel begins to twist the knife. Facing a dilemma with no easy solution, God will pursue his stolen bride. Slipping further into the pleasures and horrors of her choice, the beloved yearns for what she lost. An accusation will be made. Law will be given. And hunger for good will strive against lust for evil.

ACT III *Scene One*
WILLING HOSTAGE

Observing his plundered prize, the rebel gloated with
hideous laughter.
"He dared force me from my rightful realm, placing
this lovely, pathetic creature in my exalted place.
Now she is mine, and he plays the fool."
In a fevered binge of impassioned rage, he began to
ravish her virgin splendor with perverse delights.

⊕ ⊕ ⊕

Have you ever considered how Lucifer must have felt about
Adam and Eve? Once upon a time he had been the highest
creation in all of God's domain. No one had outranked him.
No one had come near his splendor, his strength, his cunning,
or his talent. His role prior to the rebellion had been to lead
the created order in serving and worshiping God. But he
decided to use these gifts to serve and worship himself. And
in doing so, he lost his position while keeping his brilliance.

Now, adding insult to injury, God placed mankind in the
highest position, replacing Lucifer as the object of angelic
wonder. Satan hates us because of what we are: creatures
made in God's very image. When our creation took the attention off of him, we became the focus of his rage.

His strategy for getting back on top? Mar the innocent
beauty we possess. Make us into something we were never
made to be. And do it in such a manner that we become willing hostages, enjoying our own murder.

In Peter Shaffer's powerful play *Amadeus*, the main character
is a man consumed with jealousy. A contemporary of
Wolfgang Amadeus Mozart, Antonio Salieri is an average
talent exalted to the honored position of Court Composer in

Vienna. His one desire in life is to achieve fame by creating, in his words, "Music! Absolute music!" And things are going quite well. The emperor favors Salieri and his mediocre compositions, making him the most successful young musician in the city of musicians. But then, one day, Mozart comes to Vienna, changing everything.

No longer is Salieri's position or success enough. His title and fame are hollow because he knows himself to be vastly inferior to the young composer from Salzburg, Austria. Despite all his efforts, Salieri is unable to create the kind of heaven-inspired music that seems to flow effortlessly from the heart and hand of Wolfgang Amadeus Mozart. So he becomes angry with the God he considers cruel for giving him the ability to recognize pure music but not to create it. In one of the most powerful scenes of the play, a bitter Salieri makes this accusation against the Almighty:

> *I have worked and worked the talent You allowed me . . . solely that in the end . . . I might hear Your Voice! And now I do hear it—and it says only one name: MOZART! . . . Him You have chosen to be Your sole conduct! And my only reward—my sublime privilege—is to be the sole man alive in this time who shall clearly recognize Your Incarnation! So be it! From this time we are enemies, You and I! . . . And this I swear: To my last breath I shall block You on earth, as far as I am able! (Shaffer, 47)*

And that's precisely what he does. Fueled by the desire to block God's voice, Salieri determines to destroy Mozart by burying his music and, if necessary, his corpse. As part of his wicked quest, Salieri makes the young, poor Mozart think him a friend and benefactor rather than a thief and murderer. And the more Mozart embraces Salieri's assistance, the greater is Mozart's ruin. Before long, he's an impoverished, sickly shell of a man. The envy of a mediocre man reduces Mozart to something less than he was made to be.

We are made in God's image—able to create and perform music more beautiful than anything even Lucifer ever composed. Our existence blocks Satan's fame. And like Salieri with Mozart, he seeks to destroy us. The key to his plan? Presenting himself as a friend and benefactor rather than a thief and murderer.

ACT III *Scene Two*
ACCUSATION

Intoxicated with sinister ecstasy, the rebel wiped his
   mouth in momentary satisfaction, pointed toward
   heaven, and declared in drunken scorn,
"If you are just, you will banish her as you banished
   me!
She is guilty of the same supposed crime—rejecting
   your tyrannical rule, refusing to stroke your
   monstrous ego.
A bully acquires by might what he cannot otherwise
   possess.
I did not bow, so you cast me out.
She does not submit, so your duty is clear."
Accusation made, the rebel resumed his sadistic
   indulgence.

⊕ ⊕ ⊕

In this scene, our story takes the form of a courtroom drama as the villain presents his case against God's beloved.

"The evidence is irrefutable. The defendant is guilty of rebellion, an offense for which the penalty is banishment and death. Legal precedent is clear on this matter, Your Honor. The defendant must be condemned to die. Anything less will undermine the entire system of justice established before the dawn of time."

Having banished Satan for a similar offense, God's legal obligation was to do the same with humans. To disregard his own standard would make him less than God. Sin cannot be ignored. It must be punished.

But you must not eat from the tree of the knowledge of good and evil, for when you eat of it you will surely die. (Genesis 2:17)

For the wages of sin is death. (Romans 6:23)

This was not an arbitrary mandate of an overly demanding deity. God wasn't looking for an opportunity to kill his highest creation. It was a statement of fact, a reflection of the reality that grows out of his very nature. Again, when we reject any of the good that he is (including justice) we embrace all of the bad that he isn't. We embrace separation from him, a self-imposed banishment from his presence.

Consider then and realize how evil and bitter it is for you when you forsake the Lord your God. (Jeremiah 2:19)

Evil is not God's invention. Suffering and pain are not devices within the divine torture chamber, used on those who refuse to obey his edicts. Rather, they're the reality of living in a world flawed by rebellion against goodness. They're part of our banishment. They're part of Satan's sadistic indulgence. And they were never supposed to be part of our lives.

She who was queen among the provinces has now become a slave. Bitterly she weeps at night, tears are upon her cheeks. Among all her lovers there is none to comfort her. (Lamentations 1:1-2)

ACT III *Scene Three*
IMPASSE

Head low, heart breaking, the King agonized over his
    dilemma.
"My love must respect her choice. My justice must
    punish her crime.
I can neither banish her nor draw her near.
Oh, for a remedy that will let me free my captured
    beloved."
The King's quest began—a quest to bridge the
    perilous chasm between justice and love.

The divine drama reveals to us that the great conflict of eternity is not the battle between good and evil but between good and good: the good of love battling the good of justice. And if either is defeated, both will be lost.

God is perfect love and perfect justice. Without both, there is no dilemma and no story. If God was only love, he could have simply overlooked our rebellion—treated it like a childish mistake with little importance. If God was only justice, he could have wiped us out and moved on with his life. But he could do neither because he is both loving and just. His justice had to deal with our rebellion. His love demanded that he find a way to redeem us.

Will not the Judge of all the earth do right? (Genesis 18:25)

Righteousness and justice are the foundation of your throne; love and faithfulness go before you. (Psalm 89:14)

For I, the Lord, love justice. (Isaiah 61:8)

Whoever does not love does not know God, because God is love.
(1 John 4:8)

God is love. Whoever lives in love lives in God, and God in him.
(1 John 4:16)

Before Adam and Eve ate the fruit, love and justice could happily coexist. After the Fall, each suddenly became the other's antagonist. Hence, the divine dilemma.

ACT III Scene Four
FORGOTTEN

Once pure, easily enticed by the first sensations of
excitement, the beloved now endured the repulsive
indulgence of prostitution.
Perfect beauty ravished away, blush of innocence
gone, life replaced with survival.
Covering tears with laughter, she moved from one
hollow pleasure to the next. Traveling farther down
the path of despair, freedom forgotten, she knew
only slavery.

⊕ ⊕ ⊕

A tearful young woman takes a long shower, trying to wash away the shame she feels after her first extramarital encounter. Be it the abuse of rape or voluntary infidelity, the loss of sexual innocence makes us feel dirty, violated, ashamed. But that same girl will have a very different reaction after a year of prostitution. A cold stare tells you her heart is resigned to the shame that now defines her existence. A seductive glance suggests an acquired taste for erotic pleasures. Dark shadows under her eyes and deep facial lines invade the soft, graceful beauty she once possessed. And loud, brazen laughter overtakes the gentle, pretty smile that was so charming just twelve months earlier.

This same pattern is the experience of the human race. When we were first introduced to the illicit pleasures of sin, there was a sick feeling in the pit of our stomach. Our innocence had been violated, raped by a villain, seduced by an adulterous lover. We were, at first, ashamed. But before long, we forgot what innocence was like and began preferring our fallen state.

The sad reality of the Fall is that we now crave that which should make us cry. The human race has been living in bondage to sin for so long that we can't even remember the thrilling excitement and passion found in purity. Celebrating our addictions, we view them as keys of liberation rather than chains of enslavement.

In C. S. Lewis's series of fictitious letters between two demons, the elder, Screwtape, advises his nephew Wormwood on how to use God's invention of pleasure against us.

Never forget that when we are dealing with any pleasure in its healthy and normal and satisfying form, we are, in a sense, on the Enemy's ground. I know we have won many a soul through pleasure. All the same, it is His intention, not ours. . . . Hence we always try to work away from the natural condition of any pleasure to that in which it is least natural, least redolent of its Maker, and least pleasurable. An ever increasing craving for an ever diminishing pleasure is the formula. (The Screwtape Letters, 26)

Our new "lover" has twisted the gift of desire into an affliction, driving us to things that kill rather than fulfill.

My bones have no soundness because of my sin. My guilt has overwhelmed me like a burden too heavy to bear. My wounds fester and are loathsome because of my sinful folly. (Psalm 38:3-5)

When you were slaves to sin, you were free from the control of righteousness. What benefit did you reap at that time from the things you are now ashamed of? Those things result in death! (Romans 6:20-21)

But each one is tempted when, by his own evil desire, he is dragged away and enticed. Then, after desire has conceived, it gives birth to sin; and sin, when it is full-grown, gives birth to death. (James 1:14-15)

This is the reality of every person born on earth. We all experience the enticement and enslavement of sin, pulling us deeper into the abyss of self-gratification—"an ever increasing craving for an ever diminishing pleasure." But, unlike Lucifer, we are made in God's image. Our hearts were made to experience more. Like caged birds, we long to soar. But we have forgotten who and what we were made to be.

ACT III Scene Five
SEARCH

The beloved wanted something better. Her empty, callous heart was stirred by brief encounters with enduring beauty. These faint reminders of grandeur and nostalgic yearnings prompted her spirit to seek an explanation, a purpose, a hope. Her lingering question: "What is my story?"

❋ ❋ ❋

Reminders were all around the beloved. An awe-inspiring sunset more beautiful than any gallery masterpiece. Stars and galaxies too vast to number. The wonder of weather patterns. The miracle of birth. Later, the discovery of cells, germs, atoms, and DNA—revealing a world of order so complex that humans can scarcely comprehend it, let alone decode it. All waking the memory to forgotten realities.

The heavens declare the glory of God; the skies proclaim the work of his hands. (Psalm 19:1)

For since the creation of the world God's invisible qualities—his eternal power and divine nature—have been clearly seen, being understood from what has been made, so that men are without excuse. (Romans 1:20)

Reminders are still within us. As hunger reveals a need for food, other yearnings tell us something about our original nature. We paint and sing because we were made to worship. We study and learn because we were made to know. We fall in love because we were made for romance. We tell stories because we were made for "happily ever after." Each internal reminder, each hunger, drives us to reconnect with the life we were meant to live.

As the deer pants for streams of water, so my soul pants for you, O God. (Psalm 42:1)

If we have desires and yearnings that nothing in this world can satisfy, it's because we were made for another world. If we ache for a love that no person in this world can give, it's because we were made to love someone beyond this world. These yearnings, these aches, are powerful reminders of what we were made to be and whom we were made to love.

Every human being knows there's something more to life than the mundane details of the daily grind. We long for answers, for purpose, and for hope. We sense there's a bigger picture, a better story than the seemingly random circumstances of life have told. And we're right.

ACT III Scene Six
CHOSEN

God spoke from beyond.
"She yearns for home but has forgotten the way.
Lost, wandering through the fog of rebel deceptions,
   she must know that I am here—that I love her, that
   I choose her still."
He sent a gift, a symbol of a pledge with her and her
   alone.

⊕ ⊕ ⊕

A dramatic turn of events takes place at this point in our story. Leaving her first love has given the beloved firsthand experience with rebellion, evil, and the folly of self-worship. No longer naïve, she knows their bitter aftertaste. That which was once filled with excitement has become an anchor pulling the human race deeper into the depths of enslavement. The effect? Rather than run farther into the arms of sin we yearn to escape its bondage. Seduction is exciting. But the seducer does not love. He only takes. And since we are made for love, pride and pleasure can't assuage our deepest need.

Our rejection of God's love didn't change his desire or our need for intimacy. Once we've experienced the empty life Satan gives, God always invites us back to himself, always reaches for us in the midst of our rebellion. No one enters eternal death by God's choice.

"Return, faithless people," declares the Lord, "for I am your husband. I will choose you." (Jeremiah 3:14)

He is patient with you, not wanting anyone to perish, but everyone to come to repentance. (2 Peter 3:9)

Despite his intense desire for us, God has never been pushy in his efforts to draw us back. He began by forming a covenant relationship with a representative race, the Jews, through whom he could reach all people. The story of their romance would call mankind back to lost love.

Abram, an unknown nomad probably steeped in the worship of false, dead gods, had an encounter with the one true, living God.

The Lord had said to Abram, "Leave your country, your people and your father's household and go to the land I will show you. I will make you into a great nation and I will bless you; I will make your name great, and you will be a blessing. I will bless those who bless you, and whoever curses you I will curse; and all peoples on earth will be blessed through you." (Genesis 12:1-3)

We're never told why God chose Abram over others. We only know the purpose for which he was chosen. Abram was old, with a barren wife, hardly the best candidate for fathering a great nation. But the story God seeks to tell is one of redemption and restoration. In his story, the weak will be made strong, the most unlikely will be the first chosen, the least lovely will be the most loved, and marred beauty will blossom into its former splendor. And "all peoples on earth will be blessed" because, despite the villain's scheme, "Once upon a time" is still moving toward "happily ever after."

ACT III Scene Seven
LAW

> The King's gift arrived—a letter describing a dignity long lost.
>
> It set forth the law as an invitation back to innocence, charting the forgotten path. It was exacting yet inviting, demanding yet liberating.
>
> Its words spoke of purpose and of hope. They told a story, perhaps her own.

⊕ ⊕ ⊕

Hundreds of years after forming a covenant with Israel, his first step in drawing us back to himself, God took a second step. He sent the "letter" of his written word, giving the clear light of truth to dissipate the darkness of deception. From the law of Moses to the songs of David to the prophecies of Malachi, God opened his mind and heart to a nation. To his people he gave the blessing and responsibility of possessing revealed truth. This gift allowed them to move from silence to music, from chaos to order, and from death to life. The seemingly random experiences of history were at last given form, telling a story in which we play an important part.

It told of beginnings: who we are, how it all started, and why we yearn for more. It told of remedies: what went wrong and how to make it right. And it told of romance: about the one who loves us and whom we can love in return.

The law was not given as a system of rigid restrictions but as a reminder of lost liberty. The call to purity didn't take away pleasure but infused it with passion. The prophets weren't merely warning of God's wrath but inviting God's people to experience his kindness. The Psalms did more than fill the air with music; they gave voice to the hope of true intimacy.

God's law is a two-edged sword. On one side, it makes us painfully aware of our imperfection. "Through the law we become conscious of sin" (Romans 3:20). But it also empowers us to reach for our forgotten potential. Unlike the animals, we can be driven by more than base instincts and cravings. The law gives us the freedom a well-disciplined athlete experiences when he's able to do what others would never try. It tells us we can master appetite rather than serve it and rule our passions rather than be ruled by them. To David and other writers, the law didn't appear to be restrictive, telling them not to do what they most wanted to do. It was seen as freeing, inviting them to say no to what they most needed to stop.

Blessed is the man who does not walk in the counsel of the wicked or stand in the way of sinners or sit in the seat of mockers. But his delight is in the law of the Lord, and on his law he meditates day and night. He is like a tree planted by streams of water. (Psalm 1:1-3)

ACT III Scene Eight
FIRST STEPS

Timid, yet trusting, the beloved took a single step
    down the pathway described in the letter.
Struck by a refreshing breeze, the sweet aroma of
    pleasures past, she was compelled to take another.
The most difficult steps she had taken in some time.
The most excitement she had felt in recent memory.
Her spirit leapt in anticipation.
"Could this truly be the way home?"

⊕ ⊕ ⊕

In the classic fairy tale *Cinderella*, Cinderella was a beautiful, graceful young woman. But a lifetime spent serving her wicked stepmother and stepsisters had convinced her that she was a homely, worthless servant girl. And for the longest time she was content to stay that way. But one day everything changed. An encounter with a fairy godmother and a dance with a handsome prince opened her eyes to the truth. She was not homely but beautiful. She was not a worthless servant girl but a lovely maiden. The possibilities found in those grand moments before the stroke of midnight filled her with expectancy. If the prince could fall in love with her, maybe she was worth loving. Could she be more than her stepmother had allowed? Was she made for more than the toil of bondage? Had she discovered her true identity?

Israel's encounter with the law brought us into God's true fairy tale. It pointed to a reality beyond slavery, to the freedom of our true identity. We weren't made homely and worthless but beautiful and glorious. We realized that if the king of the universe could love us, maybe we were worth loving. Perhaps we were created for more than our new master had allowed, made for more than the toil of bondage to sin. The possibilities were thrilling:

- We could be free.

  Is not this the kind of fasting I have chosen: to loose the chains of injustice and untie the cords of the yoke, to set the oppressed free and break every yoke? (Isaiah 58:6)

- We could find protection.

  Keep me safe, O God, for in you I take refuge. (Psalm 16:1)

- We could be cherished.

  "I have loved you," says the Lord. (Malachi 1:2)

- We could go home.

  Return, O Israel, to the Lord your God. (Hosea 14:1)

The first steps toward God are like Cinderella's dance with the handsome prince. They're thrilling, teeming with the hope of intimacy. But they're also frightening, filled with the risk of uncertainty. What if what we long for can never be? What if we are discovered as frauds, nothing more than worthless slaves in disguise? What if the life we seek is far worse than the comfortable bondage we know? But in the first moments of the dance, these fears fade into the background as we experience the thrill of possibility.

And then, without warning, the clock strikes twelve.

ACT III *Scene Nine*
ANOTHER STORY

Leaving the path of sinister delights, the beloved
    began slipping from the rebel's firm grasp.
"The ungrateful creature wants more than the
    indulgence I provide. She dares listen to the
    Tyrant's story.
I will not allow it!"
Master of deception, lord of distraction, the rebel
    crafted a new tale to whisper in the beloved's lovely
    ear.
"You've received a letter describing a better way?
Yes, it is so. There is more to your story than you have
    seen.
Listen, and I will tell you how it may be obtained."

⊕ ⊕ ⊕

The night of the ball may have been a wonderful fantasy. But
after midnight, it's time to return to reality. In the real world,
only lovely maidens, not worthless servant girls, can marry
princes.

While we may have been made for a better world, we still
live in a tainted one. As residents of rebel-occupied territory,
we're under the direct influence of God's enemy. And he
won't surrender us without a fight.

The problem is that we fail to realize that we're pawns
in a spiritual war. You see, when we're abused, we know it.
When we're oppressed or tempted, we know it. But if
we're deceived, we don't know it. In the battle for our
souls, Lucifer has an arsenal filled with lies. Big lies. Small
lies. Subtle lies. Seductive lies. Convincing lies. All of

them used for one purpose: to keep us from believing God's letter.

What we believe to be true will directly impact our choices in life, whether that belief is actually true or not. If I'm an atheist, I've been convinced that there is no God. Thus, I will consider myself the supreme being of my world, and survival of the fittest will be my governing code of behavior. Stalin showed us where this lie can lead.

The fool says in his heart, "There is no God." They are corrupt, their deeds are vile; there is no one who does good. (Psalm 14:1)

If I'm a polytheist, I've been convinced that there are many gods. I will work to appease these competing deities, offending some in order to please others. Ancient idol worship and Greek and Roman mythology, with their child sacrifices and temple prostitution, show us where this lie can lead.

Although they claimed to be wise, they became fools and exchanged the glory of the immortal God for images made to look like mortal man and birds and animals and reptiles. (Romans 1:22-23)

If I'm a pantheist, I'm convinced that God is an impersonal force of cosmic oneness. I will seek to reconnect with the "truth" of my own forgotten godhood and worship Creation rather than the Creator. Hungry families in India who worship, rather than eat, cows show where this lie can lead.

They exchanged the truth of God for a lie, and worshiped and served created things rather than the Creator. (Romans 1:25)

There is only one truth. Once revealed, it must be either accepted or rejected. But there are many deceptions, crafted and told throughout human history. If one doesn't suit your fancy, any other will do just fine. So when mankind received God's letter revealing the truth, it became necessary for Lucifer to craft yet another lie that would keep the beloved from trying on the glass slipper.

ACT III Scene Ten
ANOTHER PATH

The rebel twisted the story told in the letter, turning love's invitation into oppressive legislation, his captive's caring beloved into a demanding monarch.

So, accepting deeper bondage in disguise, she abandoned her journey home to take a different road.

Eagerly anticipating her arrival at the other end, the King looked down the empty path and finally returned home—alone.

⊕ ⊕ ⊕

Lucifer does not fear religion. In fact, it's one of his greatest weapons. Even God's Word can be used to advance his cause, provided his interpretation prevails.

According to the serpent's interpretation, the fruit of the tree in the Garden was not a symbol of the love God wanted to give but of the limitations God wanted to impose.

That same serpent now interprets the letter. Rather than a reminder of our lost potential, the law becomes a record of our hopeless failure. The Psalms don't express inward yearnings, they stroke God's monstrous ego. The prophets don't invite, they only condemn. Religion moves from a love relationship to a legal requirement. God changes from devoted suitor to demanding monarch. Evil becomes punishment from an angry deity rather than the outcome of rejecting good.

When the law became mere legislation, religion became our attempt to appease God rather than God's attempt to reach us. When worship is to satisfy God's egotistical needs, praise is an act of duty rather than passion. Warnings from an offended ruler drive us to obey in order to avoid punishment rather than to experience blessing.

Satan's great deception was not in getting us to believe God is dead, absent, weak, or impersonal. His greatest deception was in getting us to believe that God is a demanding tyrant who gave the law in order to mandate our submission. A God so self-obsessed that he requires all to worship only him, a God so exacting that our pathetic efforts will never satisfy him, a God trying to keep us down rather than lift us up. "After all," Satan whispers, "God doesn't want a cherished bride; he wants a groveling servant."

Believing the lie and rejecting the letter, we run back into the arms of God's enemy. And a defiant smile crosses Lucifer's lips.

ACT III *Scene Eleven*
DILEMMA

And so it was.
Accusation made, enslavement complete.
Justice requiring banishment, love seeking restoration.

The beloved yearning for home, the King calling her
to freedom.
A deceptive story told, believed, embraced.
Right turned wrong. Good made evil.

⊕ ⊕ ⊕

As the curtain closes on Act III, the light of hope is dim.

Unwilling to banish his beloved, God seeks to draw her
back. But she has chosen lies over truth and remains in rebellion against his heart. Her offense must be punished.

Lucifer finally appears on top, with both God and
mankind responding to his twisted agenda.

After sensing that there must be more, the beloved is
securely back in Satan's sadistic embrace, convinced she has
chosen the lesser of two evils.

God faces a great dilemma.

Satan tastes sweet revenge.

ACT IV

HERO'S QUEST

THE TIME has come for our hero to risk everything to win back his beloved. He will directly enter the rebel's domain, confront a lie that has been told, and pursue a heart that has been stolen. He will walk into the den of evil, exposing the terrible nature of hate and the infinite reach of love.

ACT IV *Scene One*
INCARNATION

The Hero arrived in humble attire.
Peasant dwelling, modest occupation.
Capable and confident, yet meek.
The King in disguise.
He came not to conquer an empire but to win a
    heart.

⊕ ⊕ ⊕

An angel foretells a miraculous birth. The virgin conceives and bears a child. A humble carpenter, who just happens to descend from the royal line of David, is charged with protecting and raising the Son of God. Astonished shepherds, a paranoid king, and wise men from afar. We celebrate the story every December. But do we grasp the significance that manger babe played in the larger drama? After making a covenant and giving the law, God was taking his third and most important step in the process of drawing us back.

The Word became flesh and made his dwelling among us.
(John 1:14)

God becoming human: Theologians call it the Incarnation, children call it Jesus' birthday, everyone calls it Christmas. By whatever name, it's an event that sets up a remarkable twist in our story. The King in disguise embarks upon a quest that will force the most important confrontation in history.

In any other script, the hero would have assembled a vast army to overwhelm his enemy. That's what is expected. But in this story, he does the unexpected. God's beloved, his chosen nation, was under the dominion of the Roman Empire and under the thumb of a puppet king. The people prayed for a messiah to rescue them from national bondage. Instead they were sent one who could rescue them from a deeper bondage.

This part of God's plan did not include force or fanfare. It required a quiet entrance.

> *Who, being in very nature God, did not consider equality with God something to be grasped, but made himself nothing, taking the very nature of a servant, being made in human likeness. (Philippians 2:6-7)*

How? By arriving as a baby and living as an unnoticed peasant in an obscure village. His childhood consisted of chores, meals, play, and study—just like that of any other young Jewish lad. His teen years included peer pressure, learning a trade, and perhaps even acne. In adulthood he went to work, attended synagogue, and paid his taxes. For thirty years Jesus lived an ordinary life. But he was no ordinary person.

ACT IV Scene Two
ENCOUNTERS

Healing the sick, lifting the oppressed.
Feeding the hungry, raising the dead.
Instructing teachers, embracing children.
Condemning evil, forgiving sinners.
He quickly became the object of great praise—and envy.
Observing from a distance, the beloved's look of admiration betrayed her heart—she was enticed by

his gentle strength, his impassioned purity, his kind eyes. Unable to part from him, she drew cautiously closer.

⊕ ⊕ ⊕

At the age of thirty, Jesus began his public ministry. Suddenly an unknown peasant became the talk of the town. Through various encounters, the beloved took notice of Jesus and was unquestionably attracted to him. His commanding presence, welcoming eyes, inspiring words, and undefiled passion were captivating, even inviting.

I have yet to meet a person who doesn't like Jesus. Certainly, there are many who reject his claims. But they still can't help liking him. After all, we are drawn to the qualities he displayed and the words he spoke:

- Gentle compassion

  "Neither do I condemn you," Jesus declared. "Go now and leave your life of sin." (John 8:11)

- Confident strength

  You brood of vipers! How will you escape being condemned to hell? (Matthew 23:33)

- Uncompromised integrity

  Stop judging by mere appearances, and make a right judgment. (John 7:24)

- Quiet humility

  For I am gentle and humble in heart. (Matthew 11:29)

- A sense of humor

Why do you look at the speck of sawdust in your brother's eye and pay no attention to the plank in your own eye? (Matthew 7:3)

- Supernatural powers

Lazarus, come out! (John 11:43)

In order to win our hearts, God revealed himself in a nonthreatening, personal manner. Those who saw Jesus were seeing God. As he said, "Anyone who has seen me has seen the Father" (John 14:9). And what they saw was very attractive.

When Jesus had finished saying these things, the crowds were amazed at his teaching, because he taught as one who had authority, and not as their teachers of the law. (Matthew 7:28-29)

Coming to his hometown, he began teaching the people in their synagogue, and they were amazed. "Where did this man get this wisdom and these miraculous powers?" they asked. (Matthew 13:54)

I've yet to meet a person who doesn't like Jesus.

ACT IV Scene Three
THE APPROACH

Her presence thrilled his heart as in days past.
He longed to reveal his identity, embrace her, and
   carry her away from the emptiness she endured.
"I dare not. She must come freely.

She must love my heart rather than fear my position."
Hand extended, he invited her to his side.
Reaching for his strong, gentle grasp, her hand
   trembled at his touch.
Their eyes met. In his, a love long forgotten.
In hers, a desperate cry for help.
The dawn of love—again.

⊕ ⊕ ⊕

"Suppose there was a king who loved a humble maiden." So
begins a parable whereby Søren Kierkegaard seeks to understand how God might overcome the infinite distance between
fallen humanity and his holy self. There are only two options.
Either the maiden must elevate herself to royalty—an impossible task—or the king must find a way to lower himself in
order to win her heart. His position commands submission
whether she loves him or not. So he must approach the
maiden in disguise, wooing her heart in common attire lest
she fear his position rather than love his heart. (Kierkegaard,
40)

In the Old Testament book of Song of Songs, the king of
Israel pursues a humble maiden. Her beauty hidden by the
effects of poverty, hard work, and cruel brothers, she is a
maiden resembling Cinderella. Unnoticed and unappreciated, she has been condemned to a life of empty days and
lonely nights.

But one day, a handsome young shepherd enters the
picture. Showering the maiden with admiration and flattery,
he makes her blush in self-conscious embarrassment. But he
also steals her heart. For the first time ever, someone thinks
her beautiful and worthy of pursuit. Though she doesn't

know his name, she falls in love with his strong presence and gentle kindness.

As the story unfolds, we discover that the shepherd lad is really the king in disguise. Having humbled himself in order to win her heart, he is unwilling to reveal his true identity until their wedding day. As a result, the king enters marriage certain that she is marrying him out of affection rather than duty. Had he met the maiden in the splendor of the throne room, he would never have known whether she truly loved him. By approaching her in disguise, he learned that she did indeed love his heart, not just fear his position.

By becoming a man, the King of heaven left his eternal throne room and approached us in a manner that showed we could love his heart, rather than just fear his position. He extended his hand to ours in many ways.

He announced a kingdom we had forgotten, inviting us to come home.

He called us to abandon the road we were traveling and the death we were living.

He proclaimed unseen realities, waking our spirits to the great adventure of faith. He asked us to abandon all others to join him, to be his.

And our hearts once again felt the warmth and thrill of true love.

ACT IV Scene Four
RAGE

The rebel reacted in hysterical rage.
"The one I most fear has come to take what is
   rightfully mine.

He seeks to steal away the lovely toy I have charmed.
I will not allow it. She belongs to me!"

⊕ ⊕ ⊕

From the moment Lucifer seduced Adam and Eve, he was haunted by the threat of retaliation. Immediately after the Fall, God explained the consequences.

- Sickness and death entered the human experience.

  To dust you will return. (Genesis 3:19)

- The ground was cursed, turning the natural process of cultivation into long hours of sweat and toil.

  By the sweat of your brow you will eat your food. (Genesis 3:19)

- Childbirth, perhaps the greatest joy in life, became a very painful process.

  I will greatly increase your pains in childbearing. (Genesis 3:16)

- The serpent was changed from the highest to the lowest animal.

  You will crawl on your belly and you will eat dust all the days of your life. (Genesis 3:14)

Lucifer found himself under the dark cloud of impending doom when God said, "I will put enmity between you and the woman, and between your offspring and hers; he will crush your head, and you will strike his heel" (Genesis 3:15). The statement was vague but clearly threatening: "Watch your back, Lucifer. And when you least expect it, expect it."

Unaware of how or when God would strike back, Lucifer was forced to live under the nagging pledge of ultimate ruin. So, when the offspring who had power to crush his head arrived on the scene, Lucifer had good reason to be afraid.

His strategy? To strike first. And strike he did.

- He tried to kill the Messiah in infancy.

    Take the child and his mother and escape to Egypt . . . , for Herod is going to search for the child to kill him. (Matthew 2:13)

- He tried to divert him in the desert.

    If you are the Son of God, tell these stones to become bread. (Matthew 4:3)

- He even went so far as to label him one of his own.

    It is only by Beelzebub, the prince of demons, that this fellow drives out demons. (Matthew 12:24)

But none of these strikes was effective. More extreme measures were necessary to defeat such a worthy adversary—much more extreme.

ACT IV Scene Five
TORN

Stirred by the Hero's words, the beloved spoke.
"I long for the love you offer.
But I dare not accept it, for I belong to another.

He gives me pleasures without joy, desire without
   satisfaction.
Yet I am indebted to him for freeing me from a tyrant.
My heart belongs to you, but my life to him."
Her heart was won, but the chains of bondage remained.
The Hero knew what must be done.

⊕ ⊕ ⊕

A man and woman sit face-to-face, staring into one another's
eyes. Both long to reach toward the other—to touch, to
embrace, to kiss. Despite being only inches apart, they can't.
They are restricted to communicating through the cold,
detached sounds of a telephone mouthpiece; a glass partition
keeps them apart. Surrounded by other equally frustrated
couples, they yearn for the life they once knew. But they are
separated, cut off from one another by an earlier choice to
break the law. Sterile prison walls have replaced the loving
warmth of home. Harsh prison guards have replaced the
gentle joys of family and children. Locked prison doors have
replaced a once-welcoming freedom. Seduced by the deceptive allure of sin, going farther than intended, the prisoner
can't even remember how she got here. Ashamed of the life
she's now forced to lead, she can't bring herself to describe
what she's become. But her tear-filled eyes tell the desperate
tale. Her heart belongs to him but her life to the prison.

   In this scene of our story, God's beloved sits in the prison
of her own choice and longs for what she cannot have.
Legally bound to the bondage of sin, she can only stare in
longing admiration at this one who expresses his love, separated from her by the partition of her transgression.

For the wages of sin is death. (Romans 6:23)

ACT IV Scene Six
JOURNEY

On a treacherous journey of rescue, the Hero
　　approached the towering gates of the rebel fortress.
"I must face hate to gain love, submit to deception to
　　show truth, enter darkness to reveal light."
Mindful of what he would endure, the Hero
　　hesitated, wiping his brow.
"Is there no other way?"

⊕　⊕　⊕

In the stories we love, the hero must overcome increasingly difficult challenges on his way toward ultimate triumph. But he can't claim final victory until he faces his nemesis, the supreme source of antagonism. For Luke Skywalker, that antagonist is Darth Vader. For Rocky, it's Apollo Creed. Narnia's Aslan has to defeat the White Witch, while Jean Valjean has to better Inspector Javert in *Les Misérables*.

Sometimes the main antagonist is not a person at all but an internal conflict. George Bailey, for example, resisted Mr. Potter in *It's a Wonderful Life*. But George's real struggle was within. He needed to see his life as worthwhile despite being stuck in a miserable little town called Bedford Falls. With some help from Clarence the angel, he won that battle. But not until facing the ultimate question: "What if I had never been born?"

Often the ultimate confrontation occurs when the hero becomes vulnerable to defeat. Villains are cowards, rarely fighting fair. They wait until the hero is alone, injured, without a weapon, or on enemy turf. Only then will they emerge from the protective shadows of evil to challenge a virtuous foe.

Consider God's options: Option One was simply to destroy Lucifer, thus demonstrating his superior strength and authority. In Rambo-like fashion, Christ could have grabbed Satan by his pathetic, sniveling little neck and put an end to his annoying schemes. But use of force would show God to be an all-powerful bully who must coerce obedience. Not only would it validate Lucifer's accusation, it would require our destruction. After all, we too are guilty of rebellion.

God's second option was to forgive and forget. Go back to heaven, let mankind off the hook, and ignore Satan's accusation. Why not overlook the offense and let bygones be bygones? Unfortunately, the stakes were much too high for such a simplistic solution. To undercut justice would condemn Creation to evil's cruel reign. If Jesus were to free his beloved from the slavery of sin without punishing the sin that enslaves, justice would cease to govern God's domain and would place the keys of life into the hands of death.

Option Three was to walk away, leaving things as they were and refusing to fight. If it is impossible to win, why bother? Because God's love compelled action. He could no more ignore his love than his justice. Both are the essence of his nature and both must be satisfied. Yearning to embrace us, he refused to leave us on the other side of the glass partition.

No story can end until its central confrontation has taken place. In the story of God, that confrontation wasn't just against Satan, the obvious foe. It was also an internal conflict. Jesus had to cross the final threshold, entering the domain of death itself. Was he willing to face all of the pain, torture, hate, and evil the rebel had planned? Would he scale Satan's fortress to rescue his beloved, knowing it could bring about indescribable suffering? A choice had to be made.

After a meal with close friends, Jesus entered a garden. Knowing what lay ahead, he looked for another way. "My soul is overwhelmed with sorrow to the point of death. . . . My Father, if it is possible, may this cup be taken from me" (Matthew 26:38-39).

Alone and injured, he took the cup, recognizing there was no other option. Approaching evil's turf, Jesus laid down his weapon and made himself vulnerable to defeat. "Yet not as I will, but as you will" (Matthew 26:39).

So, with no good alternatives before him, Jesus walked directly into Satan's arena to complete the most heroic quest of all time.

ACT IV *Scene Seven*
CONFRONTATION

> The Hero entered the enemy fortress to face his foe.
> "Finally, we meet on my terms," the rebel mocked.
> "How does it feel to have what you most love taken away?
> If you are just, you will punish her betrayal by condemning her with me.
> If you do not, you must restore my exalted post and bow your will to mine. Choose one—her life or your crown!"

⊕ ⊕ ⊕

In this scene Lucifer voices Jesus' choice between mankind's condemnation and Satan's exoneration. Love won't tolerate the first. Justice can't allow the second.

Since the dawn of human history Satan has been consumed by one desire: to avenge his humiliation. But he knew that a direct confrontation with the Almighty would be foolish in light of God's vastly superior strength. So he remained in the shadows, avoiding the certain defeat and disgrace of another failed attack. Instead, he watched for subversion opportunities, ways to twist and undermine God's purposes. Preferring a battle of wits, Satan sought to outsmart omniscience by luring God into a conflict that he could not win.

We see a moving reflection of this dilemma through the classic legend of King Arthur as dramatized in the musical *Camelot*. Through a pact of unity among the famous Knights of the Round Table and the rule of law he requires, Arthur establishes a kingdom more wonderful than any could have dreamed. One village peasant explains that they have no locks on the doors and the children can walk freely on the road because "we live in the England of King Arthur!" Arthur dreams of a society in which law, rather than bloodshed, resolves disputes. Arthur embodies justice.

He is also filled with love for his subjects—his bride, Guinevere, and the noble Sir Lancelot above all others. Arthur so loves these two that when the queen and Lancelot are accused of infidelity, Arthur goes to great lengths to hide the truth from himself, even banishing some of his most loyal knights. Knowing the offense is worthy of death, Arthur avoids the truth. He loves Guinevere and Lancelot too much to face their inevitable condemnation. Arthur embodies love.

Finally, the scandal is exposed. Lancelot and Guinevere are undeniably guilty of betraying the king. Lancelot flees. But the queen is condemned for treason and sentenced to be burned at the stake. Arthur is torn between his role as king and his love for his bride. He would gladly forgive the offense and allow her to live. But to do so would undermine the foundation of law and justice he embodies. Unwilling to sanction the execution, Arthur is finally confronted with the reality of his dilemma when asked, "Your Majesty, why not ignore the verdict and pardon her? But you can't do that, can you? Let her die, your life is over. Let her live, your life's a fraud. Kill the queen or kill the law."

The struggle within King Arthur is an echo of the struggle within our hero. As King, he must punish mankind's offense in order to uphold the rule of law. Anything less would condemn the universe to the rule of evil. As lover, he can't allow his bride to face the consequence of her betrayal. Kill her or kill the law. And so the ultimate conflict of our story is the good of love against the good of justice. And regardless of which one loses, Lucifer wins.

ACT IV *Scene Eight*
CHOICE

Resignation in his eyes, sorrow in his voice, the Hero
　　spoke.
"Her betrayal must be punished. Death is the price.
It shall be dispensed in the manner you choose.
Go, make ready—your day has come."
Foretaste of victory on his lips, the rebel took leave
　　to prepare.

⊕　⊕　⊕

Finally, the choice is made. In truth, it had been made many centuries before Jesus ever walked the earth. Justice had to prevail, and the law could not be ignored.

Do not think that I have come to abolish the Law or the Prophets; I have not come to abolish them but to fulfill them. (Matthew 5:17)

This law that Jesus sought to fulfill required blood as payment for sin. It had always been so. Each year blood sacrifices were made in the tabernacle and temple to atone for the sin of God's people.

From the Passover in Egypt to the glory days of King David, Israel had always associated sin with death.

• History modeled it.

When I see the blood, I will pass over you. (Exodus 12:13)

• The law commanded it.

The assembly must bring a young bull as a sin offering and present it before the Tent of Meeting. (Leviticus 4:14)

• An eternal, unchangeable precedent had been set.

Without the shedding of blood there is no forgiveness. (Hebrews 9:22)

Feeling he had successfully backed the Almighty into a corner, Lucifer pressed a decision that would condemn mankind to his own miserable fate. As smug as he had been over seducing us into rebellion and dragging us through the filth of depravity, Satan's real triumph occurred when the God who once proclaimed his love was forced to pronounce our condemnation. The sweet taste of victory within his despicable grasp, there was one more task for Lucifer to complete to accomplish his masterstroke.

ACT IV *Scene Nine*
BETRAYAL

Returning to the den of captivity, the rebel drew the
   beloved close and whispered another twisted tale.
"Are you drawn to his strength, his words, his heart?
   Don't be deceived, my pretty little toy. He is not
   who he seems.
This is the Tyrant—come in disguise to punish your
   offense.
But do not fear. Listen, and I will tell you how we will
   defeat him—again." Frightened, angry, confused, the
   beloved returned to the rebel's comforting arms.

⊕ ⊕ ⊕

Days after hailing Jesus as Messiah, the crowds turned against
him. They quickly went from shouting, "Hosanna!" to
crying, "Crucify him!" Rejecting the love of the King, they
again returned to the arms of the rebel.

Jesus' trial and condemnation were more than a miscar-
riage of justice. They were a carefully orchestrated part of the
rebel's plan. It wasn't enough merely to break God's heart by
stealing his bride. Lucifer also wanted to thwart God's justice
by killing the Judge. To do so, he needed the ultimate
betrayal, a betrayal that occurred on several levels.

The first betrayal was by the religious establishment.
Entrusted with the responsibility of pointing people to the
unseen realities of God's kingdom, they were more interested
in defending their turf. God was among them and rather than
responding in worship, they incited rebellion.

He was in the world, and though the world was made through him,
the world did not recognize him. (John 1:10)

The second betrayal was by the people. Despite all Jesus had done to show God's love, from feeding the multitudes to raising the dead, the crowds wanted more. They wanted a leader who would overthrow Rome and restore Israel to its once-exalted reputation. When Jesus didn't deliver the promised kingdom on their terms, they had no use for him.

He came to that which was his own, but his own did not receive him. (John 1:11)

The third and most painful betrayal was by his closest friends, who deserted him as the tide of public opinion turned. The disciples, those with whom he had been most intimate and open, abandoned Jesus during his darkest hours. One denied knowing him. Another sold him for silver. Most just fled, leaving him to face an unjust trial and angry mob alone.

And so, the night before their wedding, the bride demanded the groom's execution.

ACT IV Scene Ten
CROSS

Looming before them, a hideous instrument of torture, suffering, and death awaited its victim. The Hero approached the place of execution—the place of ultimate conflict, choice, and vengeance.

⊕ ⊕ ⊕

During a particularly telling scene from C. S. Lewis's *The Magician's Nephew,* the great lion Aslan informs the beasts of his newly created Narnia that an evil witch has entered their world and that he has plans for dealing with her.

> *You see, friends, that before the new, clean world I gave you is seven hours old, a force of evil has already entered it. . . . But do not be cast down. . . . Evil will come of that evil, but it is still a long way off, and I will see to it that the worst falls upon myself.* (The Magician's Nephew, 148)

From Aslan seeing to it that the worst falls upon himself, to a soldier jumping on a live grenade to save his buddies, to a mom with cancer refusing chemotherapy to give her unborn baby a chance, the essence of every hero is the willingness to sacrifice himself on behalf of another. When Jesus accepted the indignity, the shame, and the pain of the Cross, he was performing the most heroic act in history. It was the climactic choice of a life lived as the ultimate hero's journey.

> *Who, being in very nature God, did not consider equality with God something to be grasped, but made himself nothing, taking the very nature of a servant, being made in human likeness. And being found in appearance as a man, he humbled himself and became obedient to death—even death on a cross!* (Philippians 2:6-8)

So arrogant he couldn't see the strength of humility and too cowardly to understand the ways of a hero, Lucifer was blind to the real purpose of the Cross. He perceived it to be a cruel means for defeating his enemy. In truth, it was more—much more. The final threshold of our hero's quest, the Cross was God seeing to it "that the worst falls upon myself."

ACT IV *Scene Eleven*
SCREAMS

The hush of silence was overtaken by the sound of
  screaming.
The Hero screamed in pain from a broken body and
  a breaking heart.
The rebel screamed in victory as the blood flowed
  from his enemy.
The beloved screamed in sorrow as she realized
  whom she had betrayed.

⊕ ⊕ ⊕

No moment in all of eternity has the dramatic magnitude of this scene. The nail entering Jesus' flesh was at once the supreme demonstration of Satan's hate and the ultimate expression of God's love.

Imagine the hush of disbelief invading the unseen realm as the tortures of crucifixion began. Angels must have watched dumbfounded when that Roman whip tore open Jesus' flesh. They must have winced in horror at the sound of nails piercing his limbs. "Why doesn't he stop this?" they might have wondered. "One word and we could strike them down. After all, he gave them a chance and they rejected his love!" But hour after agonizing hour passed with no answers.

Splitting the solemn silence were sounds of suffering, celebration, and sorrow.

Jesus courageously endured agony beyond description. Razor-sharp thorns forced deep into his bruised head. His torso ripped to shreds from a Roman scourge, tender nerves exposed as he hung from a rough, wooden beam. His tongue parched from dehydration, he was offered only vinegar, which he refused. Hours struggling to lift and lower his body, trying to alternate the pain of suspension with the panic of suffocation. And, perhaps most painful of all, watching those he had come to win pointing, laughing, spitting, and mocking his shame.

Satan celebrated his vengeance by taking in the sights and sounds of a suffering enemy. He loved every bit of it, from the insults: "Hail, king of the Jews!" (Matthew 27:29); to the taunting: "Save yourself! Come down from the cross, if you are the Son of God!" (Matthew 27:40); to the cries of dejection: "My God, my God, why have you forsaken me?" (Matthew 27:46). To Lucifer, every drop of blood falling from Jesus' body was a symbol of triumph.

Others cried in sorrow at the realization of what they had done. As Jesus hung his head to die, others hung theirs in shame. From those who abandoned him: "Peter . . . went outside and wept bitterly" (Matthew 26:75); to those who executed him: "The centurion and those with him . . . exclaimed, 'Surely he was the Son of God!' " (Matthew 27:54); to the one who sold him with a kiss: "So Judas . . . went away and hanged himself" (Matthew 27:5); many finally realized who it was they had betrayed. But it was too late for regrets. The hero was dead.

ACT IV Scene Twelve
SILENCE

It was the blackest moment Creation had ever known.
Darkness had extinguished light. Death had silenced
  life.
Evil had murdered good. The Hero's head hung

lifeless as a smile of gratification crossed the rebel's
face. "To the victor go the spoils," he sneered.
Wiping tears of despair, the beloved recoiled at his
vile caress.

⊕ ⊕ ⊕

Every drama has its supreme ordeal, that moment when all
seems lost because the hero is powerless to defeat the villain.
In the gospel, that moment arrived when Jesus' lifeless body
was taken down from the cross and placed in a tomb. Hope
for a last-minute triumph was gone. Even while on the cross,
Jesus could have ordered a legion of angels to snatch victory
from the evil grip of Lucifer. But he didn't, and a cold silence
overtook eternity's stage.

So Joseph bought some linen cloth, took down the body, wrapped it in
the linen, and placed it in a tomb cut out of rock. Then he rolled a
stone against the entrance of the tomb. (Mark 15:46)

We mustn't pass too quickly over this scene, a three-day
pause of disbelief and dramatic anticipation. It can't end this
way, can it? Satan can't win, can he? Time will tell. But the
moment, nonetheless, belongs to Lucifer.

Imagine what Satan must have felt watching them roll that
massive stone over the tomb of Jesus. After thousands of years
driven by anger, Lucifer had finally attained the revenge he sought.
His tactics of deception and seduction had paid off, getting him
where he had always wanted to be: on top! And what was the
prize? A race of people created to dethrone him would be used to
amuse him. Like a rapist eager to ravish his victim, Lucifer turned
his sadistic attention to mankind, hoping to further distort her
once-pure beauty. "To the victor go the spoils."

ACT IV Scene Thirteen
SHOUTS

From the quiet of morning, the sound of shouting erupted.

Shouts of victory, as the living Hero emerged from death's domain.

Shouts of ruin, as the rebel saw his great triumph become his final defeat.

Shouts of hope, as the beloved's chains fell to the ground.

Just before the final curtain closes on the greatest tragedy ever known, our story takes a profound twist—unveiling God's conspiracy of grace. Suddenly, the despair and sorrow of death become the joy and celebration of life. The worst injustice in human history becomes the ultimate solution to human misery. What Lucifer thought was his own clever plot to defeat God is revealed to be God's glorious plan to redeem mankind.

*Jesus of Nazareth . . . was handed over to you **by God's set purpose and foreknowledge**; and you, with the help of wicked men, put him to death by nailing him to the cross. But God raised him from the dead, freeing him from the agony of death, because it was impossible for death to keep its hold on him. (Acts 2:22-24, emphasis added)*

The Cross was no mistake. It was part of God's plan—his means of turning tragedy into comedy. Ultimately, even Satan will serve the Author's purposes and tell his story.

Who has known the mind of the Lord? . . . For from him and through him and to him are all things. To him be the glory forever! Amen. (Romans 11:34, 36)

The Lord must have laughed when Lucifer was finally struck by the realization of final defeat. Wouldn't you love to have seen the look on his face when it all suddenly became clear? Evil doesn't come from God, but it will serve his purposes. As Jesus foretold, Satan was made to play the fool.

Jesus said, . . . "Now is the time for judgment on this world; now the prince of this world will be driven out. But I, when I am lifted up from the earth, will draw all men to myself." He said this to show the kind of death he was going to die. (John 12:30-33)

The Cross was key to our salvation. It allowed God to punish our offense without condemning us to eternal death. In the ultimate heroic act, he took our penalty, fulfilling the legal requirement and silencing Satan's accusation of injustice.

For just as through the disobedience of the one man the many were made sinners, so also through the obedience of the one man the many will be made righteous. (Romans 5:19)

But the Cross was not enough. In addition to restoring justice, Jesus also had to overcome death. The essence of death—separation from God—had to be confronted and defeated. That's why the resurrection of Jesus Christ is considered the central reality of our faith. If Jesus had not risen from the dead, there would be no ultimate hope.

If Christ has not been raised, your faith is futile; you are still in your sins. (1 Corinthians 15:17)

But Christ did rise from the dead.
And the audience cheered!

ACT IV Scene Fourteen
REUNION

Arms outstretched, the victorious King approached
his trembling beloved. "Don't be afraid. The rebel
has no more claim over you. Your penalty has been
paid, your offense forgiven, and your life
redeemed."

Eyes filled with tears of joy and regret, the beloved
ran into his strong, loving embrace as he spoke the
words she was longing to hear.

"Let's go home."

⊕ ⊕ ⊕

For the first time since Adam and Eve slipped willingly into
the darkness of death's domain, intimacy between God and
mankind was once again made possible. A satisfied justice
stepped willingly aside, allowing God's love to penetrate the
darkness of evil and invite us close to himself—an invitation that extends to each and every person who has ever
lived.

For God so loved the world that he gave his one and only Son, that
whoever believes in him shall not perish but have eternal life. For God
did not send his Son into the world to condemn the world, but to save
the world through him. (John 3:16-17)

The gospel is good news that can now be proclaimed.
Jesus Christ, the hero of history's story—God in the
flesh—overcame injustice and death to bridge the chasm
separating us from God. He now invites us back to the life
we were created to live. But each and every person must

make his or her own choice whether to go with him or to remain in bondage.

Ever unwilling to accept defeat, Satan continues his desperate attempts to keep mankind and God apart. Lies are still being told and believed. Many continue to view God as a tyrant, demanding that all bow and obey or be condemned. In truth, he's a hero, rescuing those who are already condemned.

Whoever believes in him is not condemned, but whoever does not believe stands condemned already because he has not believed in the name of God's one and only Son. (John 3:18)

But there is no condemnation for those who accept God's extended hand. He has already paid our penalty. We can go home.

ACT IV *Scene Fifteen*
HAPPILY EVER AFTER

Surrounded by music and dance, the King and his beloved enjoy a great feast of celebration. It is their wedding day. Every servant of the seen and unseen realms has gathered to share in a wonderful banquet of joy.

In the distance, screams of rebel madness can be faintly heard.

But none heeds as a song of jubilation ushers the King and his restored bride into the chamber of intimacy—where they will live happily ever after.

⊕ ⊕ ⊕

The death and resurrection of Jesus Christ are the pivotal events in the story of God, assuring mankind's redemption and Lucifer's ultimate downfall. But the wedding feast and final judgment have yet to occur. Still free to tempt and deceive, Satan continues playing the part of seductive villain. There are many sons and daughters of Adam and Eve yet to entice. And he'll take his best shot at each and every one of them. But eventually, after everyone has had an opportunity to choose, Lucifer's role will come to an end.

There are two very important future scenes in our drama. The first is when the hero rides into battle on a white horse at the darkest possible moment to defeat the rebel army and condemn its leader to eternal suffering.

And the devil, who deceived them, was thrown into the lake of burning sulfur, where the beast and the false prophet had been thrown. They will be tormented day and night for ever and ever. (Revelation 20:10)

The second is a wedding, in which each man and woman who has accepted God's proposal becomes Christ's eternal bride. The descriptions of that moment stir and comfort our yearning hearts.

Hallelujah! For our Lord God Almighty reigns. Let us rejoice and be glad and give him glory! For the wedding of the Lamb has come, and his bride has made herself ready. Fine linen, bright and clean, was given her to wear. (Revelation 19:6-8)

And so, as the drama of our story comes to an end, the glorious honeymoon of eternity begins.

I saw the Holy City, the new Jerusalem, coming down out of heaven from God, prepared as a bride beautifully dressed for her husband. And I heard a loud voice from the throne saying, "Now the dwelling of God is with men, and he will live with them. They will be his people, and God himself will be with them and be their God. He will wipe every tear from their eyes. There will be no more death or mourning or crying or pain, for the old order of things has passed away." (Revelation 21:2-4)

PART THREE

OUR PART

FOR SUCH A TIME

⊕ ⊕ ⊕

AS THE curtain closes on the main plot of God's story, it is raised on the subplots of our lives. God's story has been told, leaving only the mystery of the part we will choose to play: Will we accept or reject the love offered? Will we embrace the hero or the villain? Will seductive rebel whispers steal us away from the life we were made to live? But the individual stories of our lives are still unfolding, turning our days into scenes of a tale filled with suspense and wonder.

J. R. R. Tolkien's *The Lord of the Rings*, which became the most popular fantasy novel of the twentieth century, tells the story of two ordinary hobbits who find themselves central characters in an extraordinary adventure. Threatened by the terror of an evil ruler, young Frodo and Sam flee their home in the quiet Shire with a company of brave companions on a quest to keep the Ring of Doom from the forces of darkness. After a particularly frightening encounter, Frodo and Sam are separated from the security of the larger group. This requires each to press on alone if there is to be any hope of success. To do so, they must push through their fears and confront unknown dangers and horrors darker than any nightmare. But unlike those who remained in the safety of the Shire, Frodo and Sam see their lives as part of something more important than personal comfort and security. They see themselves serving a plot much bigger than their own. And so, risking everything, they continue their quest against overwhelming odds.

At several points along their journey, Frodo and Sam gain strength and perspective by reflecting upon what happens in the stories that really matter, comparing them to the tale in which they find themselves. Hardly a quest they would have willingly pursued, it is nevertheless one they must continue. As Sam suggests, characters in the best tales always encounter dangerous risks, and despite many chances to do so, they rarely turn back. "And if they had, we shouldn't know, because they'd have been forgotten," he says. Some heroes go on to face peril rather than a good end. At least, as Sam puts it, "not . . . what folk inside a story . . . call a good end." That's the catch. Those living in the story would prefer to be kept safe rather than risk danger.

> *"But those aren't always the best tales to hear, though they may be the best tales to get landed in! I wonder what sort of a tale we've fallen into?"*
>
> *"I wonder," said Frodo. "But I don't know. And that's the way of a real tale. Take any one that you're fond of. You may know, or guess, what kind of a tale it is, happy-ending or sad-ending, but the people in it don't know. And you don't want them to."*
> (The Two Towers, 321)

Sam and Frodo, placed in a tale filled with uncertainty, know that the stakes are high. They know theirs is an important role. But they don't know how it will end. And we don't want them to. That would take all suspense and mystery out of the story.

I draw inspiration from the reflections of two little

hobbits. Like Sam and Frodo, I'm in the midst of a tale filled with uncertainty. I know that the stakes are high and that mine is an important role. But I don't know how it will end. And I shouldn't know, lest the mystery be lost. I often find myself upset that the script of my life has not turned out as planned. But then again, maybe it has. Maybe the circumstances I least like are those most important to the story being told. Perhaps the Author has written me into a script that's about something bigger than my personal comfort and security. And so I wonder, what sort of tale have I fallen into?

Tolkien's heroes also teach me another lesson. Sam and Frodo recognize that their part, while pivotal to the larger drama, is still just a part. Reflecting upon their adventure, Sam's excitement is tempered by sober speculation:

> *"What a tale we have been in, Mr. Frodo, haven't we?" he said. "I wish I could hear it told! . . . And I wonder how it will go on after our part."* (The Return of the King, *228-229*)

They know the story will go on without them. Their quest, no matter how remarkable, is not the main plot. Their lives, as wonderful as they may be, are only subplots of a much bigger drama. This realization connects Sam and Frodo to something greater than themselves: a transcendent reality that inspires heroic self-sacrifice rather than cowardly self-preservation. That something greater enables Frodo to say at the end of his quest,

> *I have been too deeply hurt, Sam. I tried to save the Shire, and it has been saved, but not for me. It must often be so, Sam, when things are in danger: some one has to give them up, lose them, so that others may keep them.* (The Return of the King, *309*)

My life is not the main plot of reality. When self-centered pride convinces me otherwise, my story becomes the timid and passionless pursuit of safety and comfort. The humble spirit, on the other hand, submits itself to a larger, transcendent story—turning life into a passionate adventure filled with purpose. Pride creates cowards. Humility inspires heroes. And so I wonder, what heroic purpose was I made to serve?

The questions raised during my encounter with Frodo and Sam evoke other, more challenging questions. My theology tells me there is an Author of the epic story of history and the scenes in which I play my part. The yearnings of my heart tell me there is more going on than what I see, calling me to a purpose beyond my own gratification, calling me to something heroic. But when and how does the inspiring promise of a divine drama touch the trying reality of the daily grind? It's easy to see yourself as part of an epic drama while in a fantastic adventure, saving the world from the clutches of evil. It becomes more difficult amid troubling circumstances with no clear resolution, or when facing yet another day of incessant boredom. Few of us reside in a life story filled with endless excitement and amazement. Stuck in the tedious and sometimes painful experiences of life, many of us wonder where it is, exactly, that life and story meet.

Is life part of story when the baby's diaper needs changing for the sixth time today? What about when the paycheck is two hundred dollars short of the bills or the doctor recommends a few more tests to "eliminate certain possibilities"? Where is "happily ever after" when a husband walks out the door after twenty years of marriage or an angry child leaves home screaming, "I hate you!" to his heartbroken parents? Such real-life scenes sometimes cause us to wonder whether life and story meet at all.

But they do. And how we respond in the most trying moments plays a major part in how the story of our lives will be told.

SUCH A TIME

An orphan raised by relatives, she didn't have what you would call a normal, happy childhood. Barely beyond puberty, she was suddenly taken away to gratify the sexual desires of the king. The rest of the time he found little use for her, so she spent most of her time waiting to be summoned along with the other girls whose only earthly purpose was to satisfy the king's lusts. Miserable life circumstances, to be sure. But it was precisely these unhappy scenes that enabled Esther to play a key part in one of the most exciting subplots ever performed.

During a banquet thrown for his government officials and military officers, an intoxicated King Xerxes thought it would be fun to give the guys a few thrills by having a girl jump out of a cake. His wife, Queen Vashti, was the obvious choice. After all, she was a knockout—and he was proud to show off her beauty. There was just one problem. Vashti didn't like the idea and refused to come. The king was furious. So, like any good husband, he disowned her and commanded her to stay out of his sight forever.

Thus launched the search for the new Mrs. Xerxes. The king's attendants proposed a search to assemble the most beautiful young virgins of the empire into a royal harem. And so, just like that, every pretty girl in the kingdom of Xerxes was at risk of becoming part of his personal Playboy Bunny collection. Each would spend months going through a special beauty treatment and diet regimen before modeling her stuff in front of an eager king. Eventually, one of them would be given the "honor" of replacing Vashti as queen and future stag-party entertainment. That one, as the story would have it, was a young Jewish girl named Esther.

> *Now the king was attracted to Esther more than to any of the other women, and she won his favor and approval more than any of the other virgins. So he set a royal crown on her head and made her queen instead of Vashti. . . . But Esther had kept secret her family background and nationality. (Esther 2:17, 20)*

A musical bridge takes us to the next scene . . . Having overheard talk of an assassination plot against the king, Esther's uncle Mordecai warns his niece so she can report the conspiracy to the king. The seemingly insignificant detail is briefly noted in the minutes for posterity and quickly forgotten.

A sinister-sounding melody takes us to another scene . . . After years clawing his way to the top, Haman is finally appointed the king's chief of staff. All other officials are now under his thumb, and every citizen must bow to his greatness. But one person refuses—Mordecai. Infuriated, Haman declares he will not tolerate such insolence. Anti-Semitic to the core, rather than merely punishing Mordecai, Haman uses the occasion as an excuse to kill every Jew in the kingdom.

> *Then Haman said to King Xerxes, "There is a certain people dispersed and scattered among the peoples in all the provinces of your kingdom whose customs are different from those of all other people and who do not obey the king's laws; it is not in the king's best interest to tolerate them. If it pleases the king, let a decree be issued to destroy them." (Esther 3:8-9)*

Too busy to be bothered with such petty matters as geno-cide, the king quickly grants Haman the authority needed to carry out his evil plan. So a bounty is placed on the head of every Jewish man, woman, and child in the empire.

Meanwhile, back in the palace . . . Hearing about the impending murder of her people, Queen Esther is faced with the difficult choice between speaking up on behalf of the Jews or quietly preserving her own life. On penalty of death, she is not allowed to enter the king's presence unless summoned. If she simply remains silent, she is safe. But if she approaches the king to plead for intervention, he may order her death along with the masses. Faced with her moment of truth, a frightened young girl seeks advice from the man who raised her. Mordecai answers,

> *Do not think that because you are in the king's house you alone of all the Jews will escape. For if you remain silent at this time, relief and deliverance for the Jews will arise from another place, but you and your father's family will perish. And who knows but that you have come to royal position for such a time as this? (Esther 4:13-14)*

Don't miss the significance of those words. Esther is not advised to intervene because it is their only hope of rescue. Mordecai says, "If you remain silent at this time, relief and deliverance for the Jews will arise from another place." He knows that the main plot of the divine drama involves the Jewish people—so genocide is impossible. God will intervene another way if necessary. The key is not what will happen in the larger story but whether or not Esther will play the part she has been chosen to play—whether or not she will fill the role she was destined to fill. "And who knows but that you have come to royal position for such a time as this?"

Like Frodo and Sam, Esther has been given a part in a great drama in order to fulfill a heroic purpose. If she turns back from her quest, the story will go on without her. But Esther will be forgotten. Mordecai is not calling her to save the day but to fulfill a destiny. The purpose of all of the hardships she endured earlier in life (being orphaned, taken captive, and made into the sex slave of an evil king) suddenly makes sense. Esther was placed in the story as queen in order to star in one of the greatest plays ever performed on the stage of history.

Inspired by her uncle's admonition, Esther does risk her life to save others. Seeing her life as part of a story bigger than her own comfort and security gives her confidence to face whatever end lies before her.

> Then Esther sent this reply to Mordecai: "Go, gather together all the Jews who are in Susa, and fast for me. Do not eat or drink for three days, night or day. I and my maids will fast as you do. When this is done, I will go to the king, even though it is against the law. And if I perish, I perish." (Esther 4:15-16)

And as for the rest of the story . . . Esther did go to the king, and she survived. In fact, Xerxes agreed to grant her any request. Haman had built a seventy-five-foot gallows for hanging Mordecai. But the night before the execution, a bad case of insomnia kept the king from sleeping. So he ordered the royal minutes read—including the section describing Mordecai's efforts to uncover the assassination plot. The next day, the story turned with a dramatic flair more entertaining than anything even Shakespeare could conceive.

Mordecai was not hanged but honored.

Haman was not honored but hanged—on the very gallows he built for Mordecai.

The Jews were not exterminated but empowered to defend themselves from any attack.

And to this day, the celebration of Purim continues to

commemorate the intervention of a young, pretty girl who played a part in the story that she never would have chosen—but that she acted to perfection!

OUR PART

God wants to tell a story through your life and mine. Someday, when the curtain is closed and we leave the stage of time, how our stories fit into the entire drama will become clear. Meanwhile, in his grace, the Author has recorded earlier scenes for our inspiration and instruction. Each is unique, containing its own suspense and mystery. But, in certain ways, they are all the same. All remind us that every detail, no matter how unpleasant or seemingly insignificant, is filled with meaning for the story.

I've often wondered how the divine drama would have been different had certain scenes been written to suit the characters' desires rather than the story's purpose. In the story of Esther, for example, what would have happened had King Xerxes selected his wife based upon personality and character rather than base lust? Would the beautiful Esther have become queen? Would she have saved the Jews from genocide? Certainly the Author could have accomplished his purpose by ending Haman's plot in less dramatic form. But he had a story to tell, and Esther had a heroic purpose to fulfill.

What if there had been no sibling rivalry among Jacob's children? After all, the tension between Joseph and his brothers caused him to be thrown down a well, sold into slavery, and condemned to prison. Hardly a part Joseph would have chosen, but it allowed his life to fulfill a great destiny and tell a great story!

What if there had been no decree by Pharaoh to kill innocent Jewish babies in Egypt? Moses would never have been placed on the Nile River in a basket. If he hadn't been on the river, he wouldn't have been found by the princess and raised in Pharaoh's household—the precise preparation needed to play the role of deliverer for God's people. Was Pharaoh wrong for what he did? Of course. The schemes of every villain are evil. But God used his sin as a means of orchestrating Moses' destiny and telling an incredible story.

The Bible is filled with countless examples of God using negative situations to fulfill his purposes with great dramatic impact. The men and women "inside the story" may not have liked the roles they were chosen to play. But by remaining faithful amid some of the worst circumstances imaginable, they were able to play the part of heroes rather than victims. Each was chosen "for such a time" as the drama required. Each did what needed to be done. And in the process, each found the sometimes unhappy place where life and story meet.

When the mundane or painful realities of life are understood to be scenes in the larger drama, they're infused with new meaning—and your response is infused with greater import. You're no longer simply changing a diaper but sacrificing your own enjoyment for the sake of that tiny baby, unable to care for himself. It's in such thankless moments that our lives touch the drama by embracing the role of selfless hero rather than selfish coward.

When the paycheck is short of the bills and you have no idea how you'll make ends meet, will you play the role of panicked victim or determined protagonist?

Will the abandoned spouse respond as a devastated outcast or courageously cling to the hand of her true beloved, remaining faithful in the midst of unfaithfulness?

Can a heartbroken parent resist the overwhelming urge to strike back and instead show love amid rebellion?

When encountering the prospect of death by cancer, would you be able to face the ultimate human enemy without sinking into despair? Could you bravely face its cold, cruel stare with head high, knowing that your story doesn't end with physical death?

Life and story meet in these most unexpected places. And just as we don't know how our part fits into the larger drama, we also don't know how our responses impact the story being told. But one thing is certain. They do. And someday, when the whole story is told, we will see how.

MOST UNFORTUNATE

Though only a child, Shasta had lived a miserable life. Raised by a cruel fisherman posing as his father, Shasta discovered that he was actually an orphan only upon overhearing the fisherman trying to sell his "son" to an even worse master. But Shasta escaped with the help of a talking horse named Bree and headed north to seek freedom in the great land of Narnia. So begins the adventure of *The Horse and His Boy*, by C. S. Lewis.

After being frightened by a lion along their journey northward, Shasta and the noble warhorse encounter two other traveling companions who are also trying to reach Narnia: a girl named Aravis and her filly named Whyn. Along the way, the four face many dangers, including several frightful encounters with lions. Eventually, Shasta is separated from the group and forced to press on alone. Finally, he's had enough. Alone and scared, he reflects upon his misery.

"I think I must be the most unfortunate boy that ever lived in the whole world. Everything goes right for everyone except me." Recounting his various trials and misfortunes, Shasta weeps, realizing he is lost, cold, and hungry. Just then, a noise in the brush frightens the boy.

"What's that? Who's there? I know you're there somewhere. Who are you?" Shasta calls into the darkness.

"One who has waited long for you," comes the majestic reply.

Unable to see anyone and wondering if he has encountered a mountain giant or ghoul, Shasta's wavering voice pleads with the mysterious voice to go away and leave him alone. "I am the unluckiest person in the whole world!"

But then, the soothing presence of the great Aslan overtakes the scene, and the lion king invites Shasta to share his sorrows.

"If only you knew what my life has been like," begins Shasta. "I'm no better than an orphan. I've never known my real mother or father, and I was brought up by a cruel fisherman. And then finally, I was able to escape. But for what?"

After Shasta describes his many trials, including being chased by lions along the way, Aslan replies, "I do not call you unfortunate."

"But what about all my trouble? If nothing else, it was bad luck to meet so many lions," argues Shasta. "Most people wouldn't even meet one in a lifetime. And I met at least four. Maybe more!"

"You met only one lion," Aslan corrects him. "But he was swift of foot."

"How do you know?"

"I was the lion!" proclaims Aslan, opening Shasta's frightened eyes to the real story behind his miserable tale. "I was the lion who forced you to join with Aravis. I was the cat who comforted you among the tombs. I was the lion who drove the jackals from you while you slept. I was the lion who gave the horses the new strength of fear for the last mile so that you should reach King Loon in time. And I was the lion you do not remember, who pushed the boat in which you lay, a child near death, so that it came to shore where a man sat wakeful at midnight to receive you."

At that moment, Shasta's self-pity and fear dissolve into the realization that the moments of his life he most despised were the very ones being orchestrated by the great king to accomplish a greater purpose and tell a greater tale.

Like Shasta, we will someday meet the great King and Author of history. Only then will our eyes be opened to the moments in which he was the "lion" orchestrating events toward a greater purpose. Finally we will better understand how and where life and story met—the points at which the divine drama of providence intersected the smaller scenes of our lives. I can hardly wait for that moment. Meanwhile, it's enough to know I am called to play my part in the story.

In him we were also chosen, having been predestined according to the plan of him who works out everything in conformity with the purpose of his will, in order that we, who were the first to hope in Christ, might be for the praise of his glory. (Ephesians 1:11-12)

HAPPY ENDINGS

THIS LIFE HAS A MORROW.

VICTOR HUGO

⊕ ⊕ ⊕

I LOVE happy endings. When the final page is turned or closing credits roll, I'm not ashamed to admit that I want to feel good. Take a look at my family's video collection and you'll discover that I purchase the films with happy endings in order to watch them over and over again. The others I just rent—once.

A film I have seen at least twenty times, *The Sound of Music,* is so good that we own two copies! The script has, without question, one of the all-time best "happily ever after" endings, and it is loosely based upon the real-life experiences of the von Trapp family. The final moments of this Hollywood classic are, in my opinion, some of the best ever produced. Motivated by his convictions, Captain von Trapp refuses to cooperate with the Nazi regime, rejecting his commission as an officer in the army of the Third Reich. Choosing instead to flee the country with his wife and children, he must outsmart the eager and ever-watchful Nazi officials. In dramatic form, the family escapes several close encounters, including a carefully guarded music festival, a tense church-cemetery encounter with young Rolf, and the mechanical intervention of two mischievous nuns. In the end, they are successful. As the credits roll, Captain von Trapp, Maria, and seven children are crossing the Swiss Alps on foot, accompanied by a heavenly chorus—just the right inspiration to perfect an already magnificent climax. Could somebody please pass a tissue?

Just as happy endings dominate my family's video library, they also dominate my list of favorite Bible stories. I carry into Scripture the same desire to experience a happy ending. For example, I endure Joseph being sold into slavery and put in prison because at the end of the story he becomes vice pharaoh of Egypt.

I do the same thing when I read the story of David. After killing Goliath, David is forced to flee from Saul's wrath into the wilderness. Although he did nothing wrong, he's treated like an outlaw. But I push through that portion of the drama because I know that eventually David will become king of Israel.

Even the story of Job works, because after experiencing unimaginable suffering and loss, he gets back double everything he lost. In these and other stories, I find myself drawn to the ending. Just like my movie collection, I return to those stories that satisfy—while neglecting those that don't. But we must be careful about allowing our "happily ever after" expectations to overly influence the lenses through which we see our faith lest we miss the point of the story or, more specifically, the purpose of our part.

There's a minor character in Shakespeare's *King Lear* whose part is so small and seemingly insignificant he's not even given a name. The character is merely called First Servant. His entry is a scene in which an injustice is taking place: the blinding of Gloucester. He can't stand by and watch without challenging such cruelty, so he draws a sword and points it at his master. He is immediately stabbed from behind and killed. That is First Servant's entire part. In and out in a matter of minutes. The other characters have been part of the play from the start, and they will continue their roles long after his body is dragged offstage. First Servant knows very little about the larger story taking place. He only knows that in his moment he must stand for what is right. So he does and dies. But, as C. S. Lewis reflects, if this story were real life and not a play, his would be the best part to have acted, because he was the only one who defended justice.

Imagine being an actor trying out for a part in King Lear. Hoping for one of the big roles, such as Lear, you are instead asked to play First Servant.

"I'm afraid we can't use you for King Lear, but we do have a part we think might fit your unique talents."

"Great! What's his name?" you ask.

"Well, he doesn't actually have a name. He is simply called First Servant."

"No name? Hmmm. Is it an important role?"

"Definitely! One of the most important."

"Terrific. Can I read through his lines?"

"Lines? Well, you won't actually have many lines. It is more of a visual, action-driven sequence."

"OK. I guess I can handle that. How many scenes?"

"One."

"Just one? Is it a big scene?"

"Well, actually, no. You enter the scene, draw a sword, and drop dead. Shouldn't take more than a few minutes total."

Hardly an actor's dream role. But as written, it's critical to the story being told.

Of course, every actor has his pride. Imagine yourself accepting the part, knowing it's beneath your acting capacity. Rather than performing the play as it's written, you make a few alterations that will better display your star potential. Instead of dropping dead, you make an impassioned speech and transform into Rambo in tights—stealing the scene by killing King Lear and the others onstage. The audience goes wild. You shine in the spotlight. But the story Shakespeare wanted to tell is ruined.

You and I are actors in the larger story of God. Its scenes are not ours to write or alter. We serve the drama; it doesn't serve us. We may not even understand how our part fits into the bigger picture. As C. S. Lewis wrote,

> We do not know the play. We do not know whether we are in Act I or Act V. We do not know who are the major and who the minor characters. The Author knows. The audience, if there is an audience, may have an inkling. But we, never seeing the play from outside, never meeting any characters except the tiny minority who are "on" in the same scenes as ourselves, are wholly ignorant of the future and very imperfectly informed about the past. (The Joyful Christian, 70-71)

When asking God why my best friend, Don, died in a plane crash, leaving behind a loving wife and a newborn son, I wanted to know that his death was more than a random accident. I needed the assurance that this confusing scene was part of a story still in process—one I will not fully understand until the curtains close on my part and I join Don backstage.

During the dark hours of labor after losing our baby to a virus in the womb, my wife and I needed to know that the scenes in which we live do not end with tragedy. While grieving our loss, we held on to the assurance that joy would someday return to our broken hearts.

I did not, in these moments, understand why or how the present, unpleasant reality fit into the story being told. But they remind me that our ability to accept the part written for us is critical to understanding the life of faith, particularly when, as in the case of First Servant, ours is not a "happily ever after" scene.

THE STORY CLIMAX

Every story has a climax—that most important scene we anticipate in order to discover how it will end. We want the climax to be like *The Sound of Music,* prompting us to stand and cheer while tears of joy stream down our cheeks. But when it comes to our own real-life stories, that climax never seems to come. And for some, it feels more like a dismal tragedy than a feel-good fairy tale.

That's how it was for four young men whose lives were turned upside down when they were taken captive by a conquering power. Considered to be among the best and the brightest in Judah, Hananiah, Mishael, Azariah, and Daniel were ripped away from family and friends to spend three years training for service in the court of a foreign king. After learning the language, literature, and customs of Babylon, they received assignments and accepted their lots as glorified slaves. Having lost both their freedom and their homeland, each determined to serve the new boss to the best of his ability, trusting that God knew what he was doing.

Right from the start it appeared they would be used to fulfill a special purpose. Though still in training, they created a scene by refusing to defile themselves with the prescribed diet. But instead of being punished, they were honored. Hard workers and diligent learners, all four rose to the top of the class. The king found them to be ten times better than any of his more experienced advisors. He gave them new names and exalted positions. Daniel, renamed Belteshazzar, saved the necks of all Babylonian wise men by fulfilling the king's command that they reveal and interpret his troubling dream or die. He did and was once again promoted. Clearly God had destined Daniel and his three friends for greatness.

But then things took a turn for the worse, thanks to petty jealousy and kingly arrogance. You know the story. It is found in the third chapter of Daniel. The king made a ninety-foot idol for everyone in the kingdom to worship with two simple guidelines. If they bowed to the idol, they would live. If they refused, they would die.

Since we're told nothing about Daniel, it's assumed that he was elsewhere during this scene. But his three friends—renamed Shadrach, Meshach, and Abednego—were caught in the thick of the controversy. We enter the story right after they've been denounced for disobedience and summoned before a furious king.

> *Is it true, Shadrach, Meshach and Abednego, that you do not serve my gods or worship the image of gold I have set up? Now when you hear the sound of the horn, flute, zither, lyre, harp, pipes and all kinds of music, if you are ready to fall down and worship the image I made, very good. But if you do not worship it, you will be thrown immediately into a blazing furnace. Then what god will be able to rescue you from my hand?* (Daniel 3:14-15)

In the ultimate display of arrogance, King Nebuchadnezzar did more than merely order three Jews to abandon their faith. He challenged their God to do something about it when he taunted, "Then what god will be able to rescue you from my hand?"

If you know the story, resist the temptation to rush through this scene to the ending. Camp here for a moment in order to appreciate what is about to occur. For all these three brave young men know, they're about to experience the terror of being burned alive. Yet, rather than save their own necks by caving in, they respond to the king boldly:

> *O Nebuchadnezzar, we do not need to defend ourselves before you in this matter. If we are thrown into the blazing furnace, the God we*

*serve is able to save us from it, and he will rescue us from your hand,
O king. (Daniel 3:16-17)*

Again, resist the temptation to jump ahead. Remain in this
scene for a moment. Shadrach, Meshach, and Abednego
aren't proclaiming what they expect to happen, only what is
possible. They have no more reason to expect a miracle than
we would today. It had been many generations since the days
of miracles. Their recent history included enslavement by an
evil, foreign power without divine intervention. If God didn't
act then, why should he act now? Sure, it was possible for
God to save them—but unlikely. This prompts them to add
one last, very important line:

*But even if he does not, we want you to know, O king, that we will
not serve your gods or worship the image of gold you have set up.
(Daniel 3:18)*

"Even if he does not . . . we will not serve your gods."
These lines make this one of the most powerful scenes ever
performed on the stage of history. You see, from the divine
Author's point of view, *that* was the climax of the story! We
tend to look at the next scene as the climax, when God
rewards their faithfulness with rescue. But from God's
perspective, the coming miracle is no big deal. It is this
moment that he's been waiting for, not the next. And it has
been acted to perfection! I can just imagine the Lord jumping
to his feet and cheering at this point, wiping a tear from his
eye, and swallowing the lump in his throat.

The climaxes of this and other faith stories are quite different when we view them from heaven's perspective. It's not
God's miraculous intervention to save the day but rather our
stubborn refusal to lose faith that inspires even greater faith.

Our dramatic moment comes not when all is well but when all seems lost. The most profound dramatic question is not whether God will save the day but whether we will continue holding his hand if he doesn't. Again, from God's perspective the miracle is no big deal.

The book of Hebrews contains a portion of Scripture that's been labeled The Great Hall of Faith. It sheds light upon the real story being told, describing faith in the context of what we do not see. After summarizing the dramatic climax of many stories, including those who had experienced God's miraculous intervention, it also tells of those who did not.

> *Some faced jeers and flogging, while still others were chained and put in prison. They were stoned; they were sawed in two; they were put to death by the sword. They went about in sheepskins and goatskins, destitute, persecuted and mistreated—the world was not worthy of them. They wandered in deserts and mountains, and in caves and holes in the ground. These were all commended for their faith, yet none of them received what had been promised. God had planned something better for us so that only together with us would they be made perfect.* (Hebrews 11:36-40)

Yes, many actors in the divine drama play parts that include wonderful scenes of divine intervention. But many others have even greater roles, like that of Shakespeare's First Servant. While they may seem like minor players from our point of view, they are the true stars of time and eternity. And the day is coming when they will be recognized, when all of heaven will cheer.

From God's perspective, the climax of the story was not when Shadrach, Meshach, and Abednego walked out of the fire unharmed; it was when they walked in, fully expecting to die.

The true climax of Joseph's story was not when he became vice pharaoh; it was the earlier scene when he had every reason to question God but refused to let go of his Maker's hand.

Job's big moment was not when he got back double everything he had lost. It was that famous scene when, having lost everything, he praised rather than cursed his God: "Naked I came from my mother's womb, and naked I will depart. The Lord gave and the Lord has taken away; may the name of the Lord be praised" (Job 1:21).

The climax of my story may have nothing to do with the goals I achieve, the wealth I attain, or the obstacles I overcome. It may instead be found in the choices made during the hidden moments of ordinary life—such as when I decide to hold my tongue rather than win an argument, give time to my children rather than my hobby, or wake for our daughter's midnight feeding rather than nudge my exhausted wife. Who knows? From God's perspective, maybe these are the simple choices that really count and the scenes that prompt a standing ovation in heaven. It's in such moments that the true climax of the story is understood and our lives most reflect the Author and ultimate hero of the divine drama.

Let us fix our eyes on Jesus, the author and perfecter of our faith, who for the joy set before him endured the cross, scorning its shame, and sat down at the right hand of the throne of God. Consider him who endured such opposition from sinful men, so that you will not grow weary and lose heart. (Hebrews 12:2-3)

It was "for the joy set before him" that Jesus played a part he didn't want to play. Only hours before the Cross, he asked the Father to "remove this cup." But the climax of the story was his heroic willingness to sacrifice himself for others.

With our eternal destiny hinging upon his choice, Jesus accepted his part and acted it to perfection.

WELL DONE

Earlier I described one of my favorite happy-ending movies, *The Sound of Music*. It's loosely based upon the true story of a man who refused to cooperate with the Nazi regime, successfully fled the country, and inspired a wonderful film. During the same era, there was another man who also refused to cooperate with the Nazi regime. Despite the opportunity to "just get along" and preserve his own neck, this man actively resisted the evil that was being accepted by those around him. The man was Dietrich Bonhoeffer. He was a German pastor and theologian who, rather than fleeing the country, was hanged in a German prison camp. Adding insult to injury, his death came only days before that same camp was liberated by Allied forces.

Both Captain von Trapp and Dietrich Bonhoeffer refused to cooperate with evil. Both risked everything to do what was right. One lived. The other died. You might say one got the miracle while the other did not. But, as with the three young men in Babylon or Jesus facing the Cross, these stories have the same climax. It's not the ultimate outcome that defines great drama, but the choices made.

In the famous series of letters written to his nephew Wormwood, senior demon Screwtape responds to the junior demon's celebration over human discouragement. Screwtape knows that it's the times when men feel faith the least that they're most dangerous. He writes,

Do not be deceived, Wormwood. Our cause is never more in danger than when a human, no longer desiring, but still intending to do our Enemy's will, looks round upon a universe from which every trace of

*Him seems to have vanished, and asks why he has been forsaken, and
still obeys.* (The Screwtape Letters, 47)

Our enemy doesn't fear the kind of faith that seeks the
miracle or happy ending. What Satan fears is faith that
remains strong when hope seems gone. He's terrified when
we continue to trust even when feeling abandoned by God. It
is in those moments that the real drama unfolds, the true
climax of our story is known.

Satan does not fear celebration after miraculous healing
but faithfulness during chronic illness. He doesn't worry
about joy amid showers of blessing but praise while in a spiritual wasteland. Real faith, the kind that causes demons to
tremble, is revealed when God seems most absent. It shows
up when the doctor informs you that he needs to run a few
more tests to eliminate certain possibilities. It sustains you
when the man or woman to whom you said, "till death do us
part" walks out of your life. True spiritual warfare is not
about God rescuing us from trouble. It's about our stubborn
refusal to let go of his hand—come what may.

In his classic book *Les Misérables,* Victor Hugo reminds us
that the acts of justice and charity often overlooked in this
world will one day be acknowledged. "There are many of
these virtues in low places" he says, "some day they will be on
high. This life has a morrow" (Hugo, 157). It's only then
that the true heroes of this story will be celebrated, including
that eagerly anticipated moment when the Author himself
will look us in the eyes, wiping a tear from his own, and utter
the words "Well done!"

MERE FABLES

YOU ARE THE FIRST GENERATION
RAISED WITHOUT RELIGION.
DOUGLAS COUPLAND

⊕ ⊕ ⊕

SOMEWHERE along the way, my generation lost the divine drama. God was once considered the omniscient Author of our lives and of history, but he died. And now no one knows the plot to the epic drama in which we find ourselves. We abandoned what philosophers call *metanarratives*—overarching stories that explain all of life—and in doing so, we've eliminated hope. There are plenty of little stories competing for our allegiance but no one big story that can capture our hearts or explain our lives. Sadly, once we rejected the true myth, we were left with mere fables.

Describing ours as the first generation raised without religion, Douglas Coupland's troubling novel *Life After God* captures the sad reality of what it's like to grow up without a big story. Coupland introduced the term *Generation X* in the title of an earlier novel and has succeeded in reflecting the despair of this generation like few others have. *Life After God* portrays the story of a young man traveling from one empty experience to another in the vain hope of finding meaning, only to discover that he has no story beyond his own. The result? In his words,

> *I was wondering what was the logical end product of this recent business of my feeling less and less. Is feeling nothing the inevitable end*

result of believing in nothing? And then I got to feeling frightened—thinking there might not be anything to believe in, in particular. I thought it would be such a sick joke to have to remain alive for decades and not believe in or feel anything. (Coupland, 177-178)

Like Coupland's protagonist, we are a generation filled with angst—and with good reason. Instead of the divine drama of God's story, we've been living inside other, much smaller tales.

OTHER STORIES

The film *Dead Poets Society* opens amid the fall tradition of wealthy parents dropping off their sons among gothic buildings and stoic professors. Boys in crew cuts and sport coats announce the four school pillars—tradition, honor, discipline, excellence—as the headmaster reviews the grand accomplishments of what he calls "the best preparatory school in the United States." An environment celebrating diligence and conformity over passion and individuality, this campus of privilege quickly becomes the setting for a tragic conflict between old and new ideals.

The central character is an unorthodox English teacher named Mr. Keating, played by Robin Williams. His love for poetry is infectious, inspiring his rigid students to enter into the passion of life by learning what it means to "Carpe diem! Seize the day. Make your lives extraordinary!" During their first day in class Mr. Keating leads his students into a long hallway and assembles them before the school trophy case, where hundred-year-old photos show former students very much like themselves.

While they peer through the glass partition for a closer look, Keating frames their studies and their lives by explaining why it's vital to seize the day. "Because we are food for worms, lads. Because believe it or not, each and every one of us in this room is one day going to stop breathing, turn cold, and die." The boys in the photos are a testimony to the brevity of life. After all, Keating explains, each of them had big dreams, felt invincible, and saw the world as his oyster. But each of them had an appointment with the grave. "You see, gentlemen, these boys are now fertilizing daffodils."

Keating's message was clear: Make the most of every moment while you can. Life is short. And when it's over, it's over.

Inspired by his teacher's "carpe diem" admonition, a student named Neil decides to pursue his dream of becoming an actor. Tired of being weighed down by the albatross of his stern father's expectations, Neil directly disobeys him by landing the lead part in the school play. And as it turns out, he's very good. Assuming his father will be away on business during the performances, Neil figures he will get away with his deception and finally realize his opportunity to make life extraordinary.

When opening night finally arrives, so does Neil's father. Standing in the back watching his son's performance, it seems his heart might be softening to the realization that Neil was meant to be an actor, not a doctor. But that's not how the story ends. Later that evening, Neil is informed by his father that he's going to be withdrawn from school and enrolled in a military academy to prevent any more of this acting nonsense. Neil is crushed as his controlling father extinguishes the spark of passion that had entered his life. Later that night, while his father and mother are asleep, Neil loads his father's gun, points it to his head, and takes his own life. The carpe diem dream has turned out to be a tragic nightmare.

As the credits roll at the end of this film, I find myself angry with Neil's father. He's clearly the villain of the story, preventing his son from pursuing his dream. Or is he? Sure, he was strict. But he clearly loved his son and did what he thought was in Neil's long-term best interest. Perhaps the real villain of the story can be found in the "story" that was framing Neil's life. It went like this: "We are food for worms, lads. Make the most of every moment while you can. After all, life is short. And when it's over, it's over."

Rather than living in the true myth, Neil was living in a fable. That fable told him that meaning in life is only found when we are able to pursue our passions, and a life that doesn't allow us to "seize the day" is not worth living. But is that story consistent with reality? How many of the billions of people walking this planet are living their dreams? How many get what they want out of this life? Not many. Does that make their lives meaningless? Does it suggest something is wrong with their existence? Or does it suggest something is wrong with the story being told?

If Neil had seen his life as part of the divine drama, he would know that we're created for a purpose that gives meaning whether or not our own desires are fulfilled. He would know that there is something above and beyond this earthly existence. When it's over, it's not over. He would know that he was part of something much bigger than his own little story.

Neil's experience is a reflection of what has happened to Western society. Encouraged to leave behind the "old ideal" of a single, overarching story to frame all of life, we were left with a fable that hints at the wonderful adventure life can be, but ends in tragedy when we discover that the elusive pursuit of personal passion cannot bring ultimate meaning.

DESIGNER GOD

Recently, God made the cover of *Life* magazine. I'm sure it was no big deal to him, but it caught my eye. The photo-laced essay summarized the many views of God found in some of the major and minor religious movements of America. From solemn women in a Salt Lake City tabernacle, to prostrate men facing Mecca as they pray, to smiling singers at a Billy Graham crusade, the article described some of the largest faith groups of our culture, including Catholics, Protestants, Evangelicals, Muslims, Mormons, and Jews. The piece also highlighted less visible but growing sects such as Hindus, Buddhists, Holy Rollers, and Greek and Russian Orthodox believers.

Despite the many interesting statistics and pictures, the most telling feature of this issue was the cover itself. In bold, black letters the question "When you think of God what do you see?" is posed. It did not ask "Who is God?" or "Which religion is right?"—common questions of a past era. Instead, it captured the spirit of today, asking each person to define his or her own view of the Almighty. The emphasis is upon *what you think*, not upon *who he is*. Intentionally or not, I believe *Life's* headline captured the essence of what it means to live life after God. Religion is no longer a big story that frames all of life. It is, rather, a personal preference used to distract from an otherwise hapless existence.

The feature writer of *Life's* segment was Frank McCourt, a lapsed Catholic and the wildly successful author of *Angela's Ashes*. His final paragraph summarized well the perspective of many in this generation.

> *I don't confine myself to the faith of my fathers anymore. All the religions are spread before me, a great spiritual smorgasbord, and I'll help myself, thank you. (McCourt, 64)*

In other words, "I will pick and choose the portions of various worldviews that I like while leaving behind those I don't." Having rejected the one big story of his childhood (Roman Catholicism), McCourt has decided to write his own, smaller story. He is representative of those who wish to author their own dramas rather than play a part in God's.

One of the leading alternative media magazines also did a cover story on God. On the cover were the words *Designer God* and this telling question: "In a mix-and-match world, why not create your own religion?" The author, Jeremiah Creedon, suggests we embrace what has been labeled "cafeteria religion" as a new approach to faith and the truest spiritual quest of all. The opening paragraph says it all.

> *A friend of mine I'll call Anne-Marie is the founder of a new religious faith. Like other belief systems throughout the ages, the sect of Anne-Marie exists to address life's most haunting questions. If I ask her why we're born and what happens when we die, her answers suggest that our time on earth has meaning and purpose. Whether I buy it hardly matters. The sect of Anne-Marie has one member, Anne-Marie, and that's plenty. (Creedon, 42)*

The problem, of course, is that reality is painfully indifferent to what any of us decides to believe. The law of gravity is just as tough on the guy who thinks he can fly as it is on the rest of us. Either God is or he isn't. Either there is a big story that gives life meaning or there isn't. What we choose to believe is irrelevant to what is or isn't true.

But what we believe is critical to how we perceive our part in the drama. If the Christian narrative is life's true story—the transcendent myth all others seek to tell—then we are the supreme objects of God's affection. If it's not, we're something else.

The mix-and-match approach to faith has its own story. The Cliff Notes version reads something like, "There is no big story. There is only whatever fable you can piece together from the seemingly random experiences of life." It's like taking ten novels, each with different characters and plots, and ripping Chapter One from the first book, Chapter Two from the second, and so on. Hoping to enjoy a new story by reading the excised chapters in sequence, you instead find nonsense and confusion. That's precisely what we've done to the divine drama. Rather than experiencing the story as written, we have ripped random scenes from various subplots in hopes of creating our own scripts.

It hasn't worked. And many are facing the harsh reality that treating truth claims as "a great spiritual smorgasbord" from which to "help myself, thank you" is another way of saying none of them is true in an ultimate sense. But deep down, we all know that just can't be.

Of course, the Christian narrative is not the only big story around. There are others. But there are not as many as you might think. The modern trend toward relativism has made us lazy by suggesting there are far too many irreconcilable belief systems out there for anyone to compare and contrast. So we throw up our hands and either embrace the one most convenient or ignore them all. But in reality the options are rather limited.

Put simply, every worldview story grows out of some view of God. There are only three options in response to the question, "Does God exist?" Those who say no are atheists. Those who say yes are theists. Those who say nobody knows are agnostics.

The atheist, for example, lives in a story that goes something like this:

Once upon a time there was matter. Through a random series of accidents, this matter evolved into life. There is nothing beyond the material universe, and we can know nothing beyond what we grasp using our five senses. The world is a big entertainment complex that is closing soon. So have a good time while you can. And good luck—you'll need it!

This "plot" encourages us to grab all the gusto we can while we can because when it's over, it's over. That may seem overly simplistic, but what other story can be told? Without an Author, there can be no larger purpose to the scenes of our lives.

If you believe that God exists, you can either believe there's one God (monotheism) or more than one God (polytheism). Though it was a dominant worldview during the ancient days of the Greek and Roman empires, polytheistic faith is not as common today.

If there is one God, he's either a personal being who created everything (a view embraced by the three primary religions of the world—Christianity, Judaism, and Islam) or an impersonal force of which we are a part (a view represented by eastern pantheism and its New-Age variations).

If you believe in a personal God, you must ask yourself a few questions that sort through the various world religions. For example, does your God demand that we do the work to get to him or does he do the work in pursuit of us? Do we earn God's favor or does God win our hearts? It is the answer to these questions that makes the Christian faith unique. In the divine drama of Christian faith, God pursues mankind trying to set it free. In every other religion, mankind pursues God trying to redeem itself. Those stories might read something like this:

Once upon a time, God made people. He wanted them to behave themselves, but they didn't. In fact, they messed up pretty bad. So God gave them a list of things to do in order to get back into his good graces. From religious ceremonies to strict rules and regulations, God spelled out everything people needed to do in order to fix the problems they caused. And he is still waiting for them to get their act together.

There will always be another prayer to pray, deed to perform, sin to confess, or service to attend. If we're honest, we know we can never measure up. So we either give up entirely or develop ulcers trying to be worthy of God.

Again, there are other stories being told. Each has a different plot and claims to be the one true drama. But only one has the amazing scene in which the Author decides to lay aside his pen, enter the story, and play the hero. The gospel is the one plot where God redeems mankind rather than mankind trying to redeem itself.

THE BEST STORY?

According to screenplay expert Robert McKee, "Given the choice between trivial material brilliantly told versus profound material badly told, an audience will always choose the trivial told brilliantly" (McKee, 28). This is reflected in today's society, for even though the Christian narrative explains some of the most profound realities in all of life, so many choose the trivial to frame their lives. Put simply, he who tells the best story wins, and we haven't told our story well. We've been presenting our case, complete with proofs and principles, but have neglected the story.

This book was motivated by the belief that there must be a better way. I have come to realize that the true story is also the best story. It simply needs to be told.

Reflecting upon the spiritual skepticism of a new generation, twenty-something writer Sarah Hinlicky reflects,

Our parents left religion and, perhaps not coincidentally, each other in unprecedented numbers. Failed ideologies were mother's milk to us:

169

> *love didn't save the world, the Age of Aquarius brought no peace,*
> *sexual liberation brought us AIDS and legions of fatherless children,*
> *Marxism collapsed. We can't even imagine a world of cultural or*
> *national unity; our world is more like a tattered patchwork quilt. We*
> *have every little inconsequential thing, Nintendo 64s and homepages*
> *and cell phones, but not one important thing to believe in. We are the*
> *much-maligned Generation X: your mission is to get us back to*
> *church. (Hinlicky, 10-11)*

On that note, Sarah explains why she believes we will fail. Contemporary church trends, very popular among baby boomers, turn Generation X's collective stomach. It is too obviously calculated for success and seeks to be up-to-date for the sake of being up-to-date. They don't believe in absolute truth, so they reject our efforts to convince. "You're in quite a pickle," she continues. "You can't tell us that the Church has 'the Truth,' and we know that the Church won't miraculously cure us of our misery,"(Hinlicky, 10-11).

Sound depressing? It is, until you realize there is one thing left that will reach this and every generation. That one thing is the story. "We are story people," Sarah explains. Her generation was raised on movies and television.

> *We know narratives, not ideas. That's to your advantage. You have*
> *the best redemption story on the market. . . . Because of all the stories*
> *competing for our attention, the story of the City of God is the only*
> *one worth living, and dying, for. (Hinlicky, 10-11)*

She's right. Not only is ours the best, but it's also the inspiration behind every great redemption story. Every virtuous hero who sacrifices himself for another is reflecting Jesus Christ, the ultimate virtuous hero. Every seductive villain set upon destruction reflects Lucifer, the ultimate villain. And every love story reflects the relationship between God and his people, the ultimate romance.

At the conclusion of *Life After God*, Douglas Coupland reveals the ultimate yearning of our generation. Weary and barren from living in a story without author or plot, Coupland's protagonist reveals the deepest yearning of his heart.

> *Now—here is my secret.*
> *I tell it to you with an openness of heart that I doubt I shall ever achieve again, so I pray that you are in a quiet room as you hear these words. My secret is that I need God—that I am sick and can no longer make it alone. (Coupland, 359)*

We all yearn to know the Author of this story in which we live. Our attempts to write other stories have failed us. We need God.

Indeed, the divine drama is the best story on the market. Discover its plot and live in its drama.

> *But God demonstrates his own love for us in this: While we were still sinners, Christ died for us. (Romans 5:8)*

SOURCES

PART ONE

Christopher Vogler, *The Writer's Journey: Mythic Structure for Storytellers and Screenwriters,* Second edition (Studio City: Michael Wiese Productions, 1998).

Joseph Campbell, *Hero with a Thousand Faces* (Princeton: Princeton University Press, 1972).

C. S. Lewis, *God in the Dock* (Grand Rapids: Eerdmanns Publishing Company, 1970).

J. R. R. Tolkien, "On Fairy-Stories," *Tree and Leaf* (London: Unwin Books, 1964).

Dorothy L. Sayers, *The Man Born to Be King* (London: Victor Gollancz, Ltd., 1943).

Paul Harvey, radio and newspaper commentary.

Emery H. Bancroft, *Christian Theology* (Grand Rapids: Zondervan Publishing House, 1976).

Philip LaZebnik (writer) and Jeffery Katzenberg (executive producer), *Prince of Egypt* (United States: trademark and copyright by DreamWorks, LLC, 1998).

Frederick Buechner, *Telling the Truth* (San Francisco: HarperCollins Publishers, 1977).

PART TWO

Ken Gire, *Windows of the Soul* (Grand Rapids: Zondervan Publishing House, 1996).

John Milton, *Paradise Lost & Paradise Regained* (New York: Penguin Books, 1968).

Peter Shaffer, *Amadeus* (New York: Harper & Row Publishers, 1980).

C. S. Lewis, *The Screwtape Letters* (New York: Bantam Books, 1982).

Søren Kierkegaard, *Parables of Kierkegaard*, edited by Thomas C. Oden (Princeton: Princeton University Press, 1978).

Alan Jay Lerner (screenplay) and Frederick Loewe (author), *Camelot* (United States: Warner Brothers, 1967).

C. S. Lewis, *The Magician's Nephew* (New York: HarperCollins Publishers, 1994).

PART THREE

J. R. R. Tolkien, *The Two Towers* (New York: Quality Paperback Book Club, 1995).

J. R. R. Tolkien, *The Return of the King* (New York: Quality Paperback Book Club, 1995).

C. S. Lewis, *The Horse and His Boy* (New York: HarperCollins Publishers, 1994).

C. S. Lewis, *The Joyful Christian* (New York: Simon & Schuster, 1977).

C. S. Lewis, *The Screwtape Letters* (New York: Bantam Books, 1982).

Victor Hugo, *Les Misérables* (New York: Random House Modern Library edition, 1992).

Douglas Coupland, *Life After God* (New York: Pocket Books, 1994).

Thomas Schulman, *Dead Poets Society* (United States: Buena Vista Pictures Distribution, 1989).

Frank McCourt, "When You Think of God What Do You See?" *Life* (December 1998).

Jeremiah Creedon, "God with a Million Faces," *Utne Reader* (July/August 1998), 42.

Robert McKee, *Story: Substance, Structure, Style, and the Principles of Screenwriting* (New York: HarperCollins, 1997).

Sarah Hinlicky, "Talking To Generation X," *First Things* (February 1999), 10–11.

BRING THE DIVINE DRAMA TO . . .

YOUR SMALL GROUP:
Complimentary discussion guides for *The Divine Drama* are available upon request.

YOUR SPECIAL EVENT:
Help conference, retreat, or event attendees discover their part in God's story by booking Kurt Bruner's *The Divine Drama* multimedia presentation.

Send inquiries to <KurtBruner@aol.com>

FINDING GOD IN
THE LORD OF THE RINGS

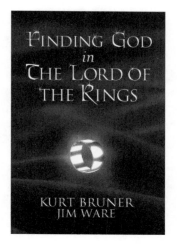

Iꞓ's been named the most popular book of the twentieth century, but J. R. R. Tolkien's *The Lord of the Rings* is more than just a great story of peril and triumph. What many Tolkien fans don't realize is that the epic fantasy, which has sold over 50 million copies worldwide and inspired the recent film trilogy, grew out of the author's strong Christian faith. In *Finding God in The Lord of the Rings,* an all-new book of reflections on Tolkien's trilogy, you'll discover deep connections between Earth and Middle-earth—and inspirational truths pointing to God's work in the world. You'll gain insights into the powerful faith that fueled Tolkien's imagination. Let yourself be newly inspired by a tale of hope, redemption, and faith against odds. Feel your own faith grow as you contemplate your role in another story—the greatest story of all. As authors Kurt Bruner and Jim Ware show us, the story of Tolkien's elves, dwarves, and hobbits is really our story—a compelling picture of an epic drama playing out on the stage of time.